encouraging creativity in the classroom

E. Paul Torrance
University of Georgia

WM. C. BROWN COMPANY PUBLISHERS
Dubuque, Iowa

Contents

Preface

The encouragement process is presented in this book as the very heart of all teaching, especially teaching to contribute to the creative growth of children and young people—or adults, for that matter. I have tried to spell out in terms of the most powerful ideas I know what is involved in this encouragement process. Admittedly, many of the ideas presented are incomplete. This is the way creativity is—open-ended, unending, infinite. I hope the reader will find this in itself exciting. It can be. It gives limitless room for your own creativity to function. In other words, I hope that your own creativity will be encouraged by the very incompleteness of this book.

In the first chapter, I have tried to show how creative activities can become central to the entire learning process. Many teachers have long sensed the inadequacies of stimulus-response psychology, especially in motivating the kind of learning that becomes a life-long process. Reward and punishment, even when they work, have to be applied over and over to keep the process going. Creative ways of learning have a built-in power of motivation—the process only has to be encouraged.

I have tried to identify only the most fundamental things that a teacher does to encourage creativity. I have included:

...... responding to the creative needs of the learner;
...... knowing the learner;
...... building creative skills;
...... building creative reading skills;
...... heightening anticipation;
...... encountering the unexpected and deepening expectations; and
...... going beyond textbooks, classrooms, and curricula.

I consider each of these so important and so fundamental that a chapter on each has been provided with what I hope will be very practical ideas for accomplishing them.

I have been greatly concerned about the special problems of finding hidden talents among disadvantaged children and youth and of recognizing and awakening this great potential. While the ideas presented in the last two chapters are directed primarily at the special problems of encouraging disadvantaged children, I believe that they are valid for all children and young people. All children and young people possess unrecognized and unawakened potentialities that will amount to little unless someone first recognizes and acknowledges them and then encourages their awakening.

I hope that you will find something in this book that will encourage your own creativity. It takes all of the creativity any teacher can muster to encourage constructive, productive creativity in the classroom. I hope that this experience will add excitement and increased purpose to your teaching as well as to the living and learning of the children or young people whom you teach.

E. Paul Torrance

To

teachers who are dedicated to the encouragement
of the creative potentialities of all whom they
teach.

Photograph by Follow Through, Atlanta Public Schools

1

Creativity and Learning

The past decade of educational research and development has brought increased recognition of the fact that man fundamentally prefers to learn in creative ways through creative and problem-solving activities. Teachers generally have insisted that it is more economical to learn by authority. It now seems that many important things, though not all, can be learned more effectively and economically in creative ways rather than by authority. It also appears that many persons have especially strong preferences and aptitudes for learning creatively, that they learn a great deal if freed to use their creative thinking abilities, and that they make little educational progress when teachers insist that they learn exclusively by authority. Such ideas open exciting possibilities for better ways of individualizing instruction and educating a larger proportion of people to a higher level (Torrance, 1965a; Taylor, 1968).

Learning creatively takes place in the process of becoming sensitive to or aware of problems, deficiencies, gaps in knowledge, missing elements, disharmonies, and so on; bringing together in new relationships available existing information; defining the difficulty of identifying the missing elements; searching for solutions, making guesses, or formulating hypotheses about the problems or deficiencies; testing and retesting these hypotheses and modifying and retesting them; perfecting them; and finally, communicating the results. This is a natural, healthy human process. Strong human motivations are involved at each stage.

In school, sensitivity to problems, gaps in information, deficiencies, and disharmonies may be aroused either by a structured sequence of learning experiences designed, planned, and directed by the teacher or by the self-initiated activities of an individual learner or group of learners. Regardless of the source of the arousal, sensing an incompleteness, a disharmony, or a problem arouses tension or motivation. The learner is uncomfortable. He is "curious," has a "divine discontent," or recognizes a "need." The learner wants to relieve his tension. Since he

1

has no adequate learned response, or because his habitual ways of responding are inadequate, he searches both in his own memory storehouse and in other resources, such as books and the experiences of others, for possible answers. From these, he tries to identify the gap in information or to define the problem. This achieved, he searches for possible alternative solutions, diagnosing, manipulating, rearranging, building onto previous experience, and making guesses or approximations. Until these guesses or hypotheses are tested, modified, and retested, the learner is still uncomfortable and is motivated to continue the process. He continues trying to perfect his solution until it is logically and aesthetically satisfying. The tension remains unrelieved, however, until the learner communicates in some way his discoveries, solutions, or productions.

Some educators would say that this is nothing more than a problem-solving process and that it does not necessarily involve creativity. According to my interpretation, this process almost always involves some degree of creativity, but the degree varies greatly from one situation to another. I regard creativity as a special kind of problem solving and like the criteria suggested by Newell, Shaw, and Simon (1962) for assessing the degree of creativity involved in problem solving. In creative thinking, the product of thinking has novelty and value, either for the thinker or for his culture. The problem as initially presented was vague and undefined, so that the statement of the problem itself had to be formulated. The thinking involved requires high motivation and persistence and is unconventional in the sense that it requires modification or rejection of previously accepted ideas. Also quite useful are Selye's (1962) criteria which require that the product of creative thinking be true, generalizable, and surprising in the light of what the learner knew at the time the thinking occurred.

Learning by authority occurs when the learner is told what he should learn and when he accepts something as true because an authority says that it is. The authority may be a classroom teacher, a parent, an expert in the special field, a textbook, a newspaper, or a reference book. Frequently, it is majority opinion, the consensus of the peer group.

Learning by authority appears primarily to involve such abilities as recognition, memory, and logical reasoning—which are, incidentally, the abilities most frequently assessed by traditional intelligence tests and measures of scholastic aptitude. In contrast, learning creatively through creative and problem-solving activities, in addition to recognition, memory, and logical reasoning, requires such abilities as evaluation (especially the ability to sense problems, inconsistencies, and missing elements), divergent production (e.g., fluency, flexibility, originality, and elaboration), and redefinition. Guilford (1968) and others who have been concerned about the assessment and development of these abilities look upon each of these abilities as a distinct kind of thinking skill. They believe that if we know what kinds of skills are involved in creative thinking, we have a much more definite objective at which to aim in teaching how to think creatively. Guilford believes that an awareness of the abilities in his structure of intellect model will give the teacher far better guidance than the stimulus-response models of learning that have dominated educational psychology. For comprehensive treatments of Guilford's structure of intellect model, the reader should consult Guilford's *The Nature of Human Intelligence* (1967) and Meeker's *The Structure of Intellect: Its Interpretation and Uses* (1969).

Now, I shall present two examples of creative and problem-solving activities that I have conducted with five-year-old children being taught under the Creative-Aesthetic Approach to School Readiness and Beginning Reading and Arithmetic (Torrance, Fortson, and Diener, 1968; Torrance and Fortson, 1968; Torrance, 1968). In presenting these illustrative examples, I shall try to show how learning processes are involved and how different intellectual skills are developed. Then, I shall point out what I regard as the fundamental characteristics of educational experiences that involve the learning processes in creativity and problem solving.

Illustrative Activities

Magic Net and Problem Solving in Creative Dramatics

The use of the "Magic Net" in problem solving in creative dramatics to involve the learning processes was developed first through my work with disadvantaged children from ages six through thirteen. Many of the children with whom I worked exhibited strong feelings of fear and either refused to attempt roles in creative dramatics or were unable to play roles with any degree of skill. One device developed to cope with this difficulty was the use of "Magic Net," pieces of 36" x 72" nylon net in various colors. I used it to create an atmosphere of magic in which the children could imaginatively become whatever they wished. Usually, I would give six to ten of them each a piece of the net and ask them to choose some role—some person, animal, or other being that they wanted to become. Then, they were asked in turn while wearing the net to stand, walk, and dance like the person, animal, or other being they had chosen to become. Next, the entire group would begin making up a story, using the roles chosen by the children with the "Magic Nets." The role players then enacted in pantomime the story as it was told by the audience.

This situation posed challenging problems to both the actors and the storytellers. The first problem was to think of situations that would involve the characters chosen by the actors. As each storyteller added his bit, the problem of each successive storyteller became one of continuing the action already initiated or of extricating the hero from a predicament. The problem of the actors was to interpret through movement or pantomime the actions related by the storytellers.

An interesting characteristic found among the disadvantaged children was the tendency to choose the same role that their peers had chosen. If one girl chose to be a queen, all the girls would choose to become queens, and all the boys would choose to become kings. They seemed to have an exceedingly strong need for the support of their peers, even with the "protection" of the "Magic Net." Thus, it became a problem for storytellers to create stories with five queens and kings, or with five witches and five old men. Even when a child chose a unique role, it was sometimes necessary to reinforce him with other children in the same role.

On a few occasions, an immediate sequel to these creative problem-solving dramatics was that each child (both actors and audience) was motivated to write or to tell to an adult an imaginative story which continued the dramatic narrative from its terminal predicament; or else to elaborate upon a particular incident in the drama.

A few adaptations were invented in the application of this technique to five-year-old children in the Creative-Aesthetic Approach. The number of characters was limited to six or fewer. Each storyteller contributed only one incident, and this was enacted immediately. Then the next storyteller resumed with the problem where the previous storyteller had left it. It was also discovered that it was useful to provide the storyteller with a "Magic Net." This identified the storyteller and prevented the confusion of having three or four storytellers at the same time. It also helped markedly in enabling the storyteller to overcome inhibitions and blocking. Previously with five-year-olds, I would find that eager volunteers became speechless when called upon to become storytellers. The use of the "Magic Net" practically overcame this difficulty and resulted in greater fluency and originality.

Typically, what kind of learning occurs in experiences of this type? The information giving and information acquiring in this kind of creative and problem-solving activity depends a great deal upon the nature of the characters chosen by the actors, the experiences of the storytellers and the actors, the problems created by the storytellers, and the interpretations of the actors. If the characters are animals, the activity usually results in the sharing of information about the characteristics and behavior of animals. If occupational roles are chosen, the content involves concepts and experiences in the occupational world. If family roles are chosen, the content becomes family relationships and problem solving. If fantasy roles are chosen, the subject matter becomes the literature from which these roles come. Almost always, there is practice in human relationships, psychomotor skills, and social skills. The leader may introduce guidance that contributes to improved observation skills, to forming and testing hypotheses, to elaborating an idea, to verbal fluency, and to originality.

It will be observed that there is a tendency to involve the child's entire being—his intellect, emotions, physical action, and so forth. Thus, there are opportunities for the alert teacher to encourage the particular kinds of learning that meet the needs of the children involved. For example, in the work with disadvantaged children, one episode provided an opportunity to help Pamela learn a more favorable self-concept. Pamela was an exceedingly timid six-year-old Negro girl who had failed in the first grade. On one occasion, Pamela chose to be a bear in one of the princess stories. Neither the magic of the net nor my encouragement were powerful enough to help her fulfill the role of the bear. The magic came when I assigned three aggressive young boys to support her in this role and be bears with her. Then she played the role of the bear with enthusiasm, actually frightening the princesses at their party.

Pamela's adult sponsor commented as follows concerning her behavior that day:

> Pamela had been so quiet and had not been a part of the creative drama, dance, song, or play until today. She was given a "Magic Net" and decided to be a bear. She was too timid and withdrawn to be a good bear, even with encouragement. Dr. Torrance, realizing this, reinforced her with some more bear children. She became an excellent bear. She overcame some of her shyness and began to interact with the group, not just in play acting. Her success seemed to change her whole self-image. Pamela, with her quiet voice, entered into the group problem-finding game and gave very intelligent problems. She was anxious to participate and to contribute to the group . . . I saw a sense of achievement in her approach.
>
> Earlier, I could not get her to concentrate and study the picture when I gave her the Picture Interpretation questions. But today, she would look at the pictures and study them. She was able to make up an entire story of Smokey Bear from the pictures. I was amazed that she knew so much. . . . I found today that she is far more intelligent than I had dreamed. She lacks confidence, and being unsure and inhibited can be taken for signs of low intelligence. But when the inhibition is broken, you can see that she is not dull but just too afraid to exert and show her abilities.

Just Imagine

In the Just Imagine exercises that I have developed, several kinds of techniques are used for engaging children in creativity and problem solving involving learning processes. Basically, I guide the children in producing something and then doing something with what they have produced. Let me describe a fairly typical pattern.

In one of these exercises, the children were shown an attractive original drawing of a pond with frogs, lily pads, and insects. The children were asked just to imagine that they could enter into the life of the pond and become anything in the pond that they wanted to be. Each child was then asked to choose what he wanted to be in the life of the pond. As a result, we had frogs, alligators, a crocodile, fish, mosquitoes, water, sticks, tree roots at the bottom of the pond, and even the fog that rises over the pond some mornings. Then we created the drama of life in the pond. The frogs jumped, croaked, and sang their song. The alligator entered the pond and the jumping and croaking stopped; we paused to wonder why. The fog came over the pond, and we wondered how this made the frogs, fish, and other living things feel. The crocodile mistakenly attacked the root of the tree at the bottom of the pond, and we paused to wonder why he made this mistake.

Immediately after this dramatic creation by a group of twenty-four children, they were asked to draw some event that might occur if they could enter the life of the pond. Later, the experience was used as a basis for writing songs and stories which were then placed on reading charts and used as reading materials for the class, for singing, and for creative movement. The situation was also used for teaching number facts. They enacted problems such as the following: "If there are three frogs on the log and three frogs on the bank, how many will there be in the pond if they all jump in? If three of them jump out, how many will be left in the pond?"

After explorations such as these, one class was encouraged to make more elaborate paintings of something that happened in the pond. In the other class, a giant mural of the pond was painted. Each child then constructed, painted, and placed in the pond whatever he desired. The initial drawing and painting of life in the pond presented the children with difficult problems. For example, how do you draw and paint the animals in the pond and then add water so that it does not cover up the animals and hide them? Some go ahead and cover their animals. Some color around them. Some avoid painting any water at all or use a light color. Some draw the animals on top of the water or jumping out of the water. Some draw water but no animals. Later, they discussed their solutions and thought of better ones.

Characteristics of Activities

What are the fundamental characteristics of creative and problem-solving activities that involve the learning processes? I have identified three characteristics that I believe are fundamental in creative and problem-solving activities to motivate and activate the learning processes.

Incompleteness, Openness

Perhaps the most fundamental characteristic of activities that involve the learning processes through creativity and problem solving is incompleteness or openness. Many outstanding creative people have commented upon the power of incompleteness in motivating learning and achievement. Ben Shahn (1959), in discussing his creativity in painting, described how he traps images just as some inventors trap ideas for inventions. He explained that these images are not complete, saying, "If I had a complete image, I think I would lose interest in it." To him, the most rewarding thing about painting is the exploration and the discovery.

A child may encounter incompleteness outside of school, and this may motivate his learning; or he may encounter it in the classroom. The incompleteness may be encountered in pictures, stories, objects of instruction, teacher or pupil questions, the behavioral settings of the classroom or playground, or in structured sequences of learning activities. I encourage children to see all information as being incomplete. I show a picture or read a story and then ask them to think of all the things they would like to know that the picture or the story does not tell them. I then encourage them to ask questions about these things.

There are many teacher strategies for creating and/or using incompleteness to motivate the learning processes and keep them going. I have attempted to identify the strategies that might be used for this purpose before, during, and after a reading lesson, a science lesson, an art lesson, or whatever. The following strategies are usually effective prior to a lesson, an assignment, or other learning activity:

1. Confrontation with ambiguities and uncertainties.
2. Heightened anticipation and expectation.
3. The familiar made strange or the strange made familiar by analogy.
4. Looking at the same thing from several different psychological, sociological, physical, and emotional viewpoints.
5. Provocative questions requiring the learner to examine information in new ways.
6. Predictions from limited information required.
7. Tasks structured only enough to give clues and direction.
8. Encouragement to take the next step beyond what is known.

During the process of a lesson, the following strategies seem useful:

1. Continued heightening of anticipation and expectation.
2. Encouragement of the creative and constructive rather than cynical acceptance of limitations.
3. Exploration of missing elements and possibilities made systematic and deliberate.
4. Juxtaposition of apparently irrelevant or unrelated elements.
5. Mysteries and puzzles explored and examined.
6. Open-endedness preserved.
7. Ongoing predictions from limited information as new facts are acquired.
8. Surprises heightened and deliberately used.
9. Visualization of events, places, etc. encouraged.

The following strategies seem especially appropriate following a lesson, an assignment, or the like:

1. Ambiguities and uncertainties played with.
2. Constructive response called for (a better way, a more beautiful effect, etc.).
3. Digging deeper, going beyond the obvious, encouraged.
4. Elaborating some element through drawings, dramatics, imaginative stories, and the like.
5. Search for elegant solutions encouraged (i.e., the solution that takes into account the largest number of variables).
6. Experimentation and testing of ideas encouraged.
7. Future projections encouraged and improbabilities entertained.
8. Multiple hypotheses encouraged.
9. Reorganization and reconceptualization of information required.
10. Syntheses of diverse and apparently irrelevant elements required.
11. Transforming or rearranging information or other elements.
12. Taking the next step beyond what is known.

These and other strategies will be illustrated and discussed at length in Chapters 6, 7, and 8.

Producing Something and Using It

My own favorite way of involving the learning processes in creativity and problem solving is to have the learner produce something of his own—a drawing, a story, a sculptured animal—and then to do something with what he has produced. This was a central feature of both the illustrative activities described earlier. It is also a central feature of the ideabooks for elementary and junior high school pupils created by Myers and Torrance (1964, 1965ab, 1966ab) and the Imagi/Craft materials created by Cunnington and Torrance (1965).

In the ideabooks, there are three levels of involvement. The initiating activity allows the learner to work with his classmates in producing ideas. He then thinks more deeply on his own about the subject. At the third level, he is encouraged to do something with what he produced at the second level.

In the Imagi/Craft materials, varieties of techniques are employed. In *Sounds and Images,* the child is asked to record the word pictures of the images generated to each of four sounds. He is then asked to listen to these same four sounds a second and a third time, each time stretching his imagination farther.

Finally, he is asked to select his most interesting image and use it as the basis for a story, a painting, a song, or a dance. In several of the recorded dramatizations, the recording is stopped at strategic points for problem solving, predictions, and the consideration of various possibilities. These are then used as the basis for further inquiry, research, or productions such as dramas, poems, stories, or songs.

Using Pupil Questions

The child's "wanting to know" is reflected in the number and kinds of questions he asks. By the time a child enters school for the first time, he is on his way to learning the skills of finding out by asking questions. When he enters school, however, the teacher usually begins asking all of the questions, and the child has little or no chance to ask any. Furthermore, the teacher's questions are rarely asked to gain information. The teacher almost always knows the answer. Questions for information are rare in the classroom. Just imagine how stimulating it would be if teachers really asked children for information! If teachers did this, children would doubtless ask questions far more freely and with greater skill and excitement.

Asking questions that the teacher cannot answer should be accepted as normal and desirable, coming out of a mutual searching for the truth.

Fundamental to the development of better questioning skills is the teacher's ability to be respectful of the questions children ask and to help them achieve the skills for finding the answers. Nothing is more rewarding to the child who asks a question than to find the answer. This does not mean that the teacher must answer the question immediately or answer it at all. Perhaps it would be a good rule never to tell a child something he can find out for himself. This does not mean that answering questions should be postponed. Teachers should learn how to enrich the moments between the asking of the question and the finding of the answer.

Guiding Learning in Creativity and Problem Solving

The necessity for teacher guidance of learning in creativity and problem solving should already be obvious. Unless there is guidance and direction from a teacher, most children will cease to develop after a certain stage and will become discouraged. Creative ways of learning, in fact, call for the most sensitive kind of guidance and direction possible. They call for intense listening and observing, and for giving the kind of guidance that will make all honest efforts to learn worthwhile enough to sustain motivation and to keep the learning process going. There are times when the teacher must deal with the disparagement, ridicule, and criticism of other children. Once motivation has taken place, however, it is both difficult and dangerous to stop the learning process.

An Exercise

To test out the appeal of the incomplete task, try out the exercise on the next page with a dozen or so of your friends or with a class. Ask them which of the two exercises (the incomplete one or the one calling for an improvement) they would prefer. Or, better, make up some sheets with these exercises and see which one they will choose. With several hundred people, I have found that over 80 percent chose the incomplete task.

Choose One of These Tasks

1. Complete this figure in such a way as to make an interesting picture. Add details to make it tell an interesting story.

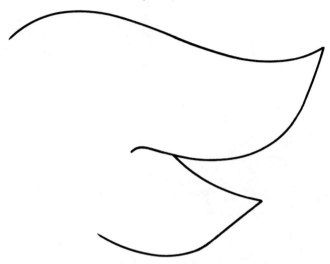

2. Add to this sketch of a stuffed toy dog some improvement that you think will make it more interesting to play with.

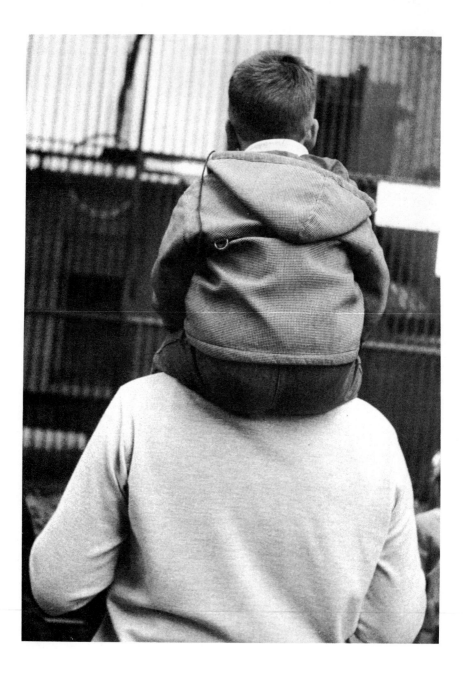

2

Respondinding
to Creative Needs

Creativity is encouraged in the classroom whenever teachers and pupils respond to one another's creative needs. Thus, teachers should be able to identify and understand the creative needs of children. Although our knowledge and understanding of children's creative needs are incomplete, our increased understanding of the creative process, the nature of the creative person, the nature of the mental abilities involved in behaving creatively, and the conditions that facilitate and inhibit creative behavior makes it possible to look with new perspective at creative needs. The power of man's creative needs is obvious in the definition of the creative process given in the preceding chapter.

To review, we have found that it is easy to see that strong human needs are involved in each stage of the creative thinking process. If we sense something missing or out of harmony, tension is aroused. We are uncomfortable, and we want to do something to relieve the tension. This makes us search for possible solutions, ask questions, and make guesses. We are still uncomfortable because we realize that our guesses may be incorrect, and we want to find out if they are true. Therefore, we are driven to experiment and to test them, to correct our errors and to modify our guesses. We cannot tolerate too much uncertainty. Once we discover something, we are still uncomfortable until we can tell somebody about it or until we can use it in some constructive way. This is one of the reasons that it is so natural for children to want to learn in creative ways.

Although creative needs and creative thinking abilities are universal enough to make creative ways of learning valuable for all children, there are great individual differences in the strength of these needs and the degree and nature of these abilities. Thus, the creative way of learning must not be regarded as the exclusive way of learning for all children—nor for any single child. Children also need the anchors in reality, or guides to behavior, that come from learning by authority.

No method of instruction seems to be the best one for all children. Even some of the most successful experiments in education show that some children fail to profit by the experimental procedure. And yet it is an overwhelming task for a teacher to tailor-make the educational experiences for every child in terms of his unique constellation of needs, abilities, interests, and personality characteristics. It should help us that we know now a few bases upon which individualization can be accomplished. I would like to use an analogy to develop this concept somewhat further.

There is an analogy between our problem and the difference in the ways in which cats and dogs learn. When I was a child, my pets were dogs. Somehow, I managed to train them so that they became reasonably well-behaved, apparently happy, affectionate, and loyal pets, as well as productive killers of rats, mice, and moles. My teaching skills did not match those of the instructors in Dog Obedience Schools, but I think my methods were basically similar to those used in the Obedience School. Essentially, I punished undesirable behavior and rewarded desirable behavior. Dogs, apparently anxious by nature to please, respond to this kind of treatment.

In recent years, my pets have been cats. I undertook to train Hazel, my first cat, in very much the same way that I had, as a child, trained my dogs. In time, I gained insight into the ways in which cats learn, and I adapted my treatment of Hazel accordingly. She became a well-behaved apparently happy, loyal, and productive cat. She must have set some kind of record for the capture of mice and shrews. She was infinitely curious, independent, proud (sometimes appearing haughty and self-satisfied), possessed of great dignity; she was manipulative, experimental, playful, quiet, timid and shy, adventurous, highly sensitive to ridicule or criticism, energetic, persistent, and yet affectionate and considerate.

Hilda, the second cat, was trained according to my new understanding of the cat's way of learning. When she and the other kittens in the litter first chose to use a different corner of the basement for their toilet than the one I had intended, I provided facilities in the corner which they had chosen. Formerly, I would have punished them in order to force them to use the location I had chosen. Later, they started using the facilities which had been established for Hazel. Hilda has never scratched me, and yet she puts to flight hostile cats far larger than she is. She has never been difficult. Her greatest delinquency is that she pulls books from the shelves when she is frustrated or angry with my wife or me. We can assess the degree of her provocation by the number of books she pulls down. If we respect her need to express her frustration in this harmless way and simply place the books back on the shelf, all goes well. Creative children need the freedom to be themselves to this same extent.

It is my belief that the reason highly creative children frequently become difficult children is that we have been unwilling to recognize fundamental differences in needs and in ways of learning among children—ways which are as fundamentally different as the ways by which cats and dogs learn. In the main, dogs tend to learn by authority. They are anxious to please and to respond favorably to the stimuli provided. Cats, on the other hand, tend to learn creatively—by exploring, testing the limits, searching, manipulating, and playing. They have been noted throughout history for their curiosity and venturesomeness. This is (I believe) the basis for the tremendous differences in the ways by which cats and dogs learn. This does not mean that dogs are lacking in curiosity and that they learn exclusively in deliberate ways, by authority. Dogs also learn spontaneously, in creative ways. Similarly, cats do not learn exclusively through spontaneous ways. They respond to firm limits and deliberate methods to some extent. There are big differences, however, in preferred ways of learning. Similarly, I believe that one of the most fundamental ways in which children differ in their ways of learning springs from the relative strengths of their creative needs.

The cat and the creative child both need a *responsive environment* rather than just a stimulating one. Many teachers and parents ask, "What can we do to stimulate creativity?" It is not necessary to stimulate the creative child to think creatively, although it may be necessary to provide a stimulating environment for the child who prefers to learn by authority and for the child whose creative needs have been suppressed for a long time. With the creative child, the adult must avoid throwing that child's thinking processes off course, but instead, guide him by providing a responsive environment. It is my belief that this approach will lead to the controlled kind of freedom which seems to be necessary for productive, creative behavior.

What Are Some of the Creative Needs?

The nature of some of the creative needs is obvious from the definition I have already given. It should be clear that the creative needs are those which lead us to respond constructively to new situations, rather than merely to adapt or adjust to new or existing situations. This, in turn, makes clear that the true value of creativity is to be found in daily living, not just in the creation of new products.

Let us look now more specifically and in somewhat greater depth at some of the creative needs.

Curiosity Needs

One of the most impelling of a child's creative needs is his curiosity. The way his environment treats these curiosity needs determines in a large measure how a child will develop and use his creative potentialities.

A common characteristic of the creative child is his persistent tendency to ask questions about the things that puzzle him. Since he is attracted to the puzzling, the unknown, and the unusual, his questions are many and are frequently embarrassing. My associates and I have now assembled data from about twelve states and nine countries outside the United States (India, Western Samoa, Germany, Canada, Australia, Malaya, the Philippines, Mexico, and Greece) concerning the characteristics of the ideal child. (A copy of the *revised* 66-item checklist is contained in Appendix A.) "Always asking questions" ranks uniformly rather low among the sixty-two characteristics included in the checklist, thirty-ninth among both parents and teachers in the United States. Subjects were asked to check each of the sixty-two characteristics that they considered desirable, to double check the five most important characteristics, and to draw a line through all characteristics considered undesirable. Rankings were determined by assigning a weight of two for a double check, one for a single check, and minus one for characteristics having a line drawn through them. Only in Western Samoa was the ranking for "always asking questions" better than thirty-first. To the Samoan teacher, however, "always asking questions" means asking if what they have done is all right or if what they are doing is what the teacher wants done. Even asking for permission to do something is disfavored, and sometimes strongly punished. One of the reasons "asking questions about puzzling phenomena" causes a child to be considered so difficult is that such questions disturb carefully planned classroom procedures and organization.

Of the sixty-two characteristics in the ideal pupil checklist, the most universally discouraged and punished is "disturb class procedures or organization." Only in Greece and Western Samoa does this characteristic fail to be among the one or two most disliked characteristics of children (fifty-eighth in Greece and fifty-third in Western Samoa).

Even among the most creative geniuses in modern history, cruel punishment sometimes resulted from their tendency to ask questions about puzzling phenomena. Thomas A. Edison's teacher did not like the kind of questions Tom asked. As a consequence, the boy spent many mornings sitting on the low stool in the corner of the schoolroom during the three months he attended school. After three months, the teacher decided that young Tom was mentally "addled." He became enraged one morning when Tom, observing that a certain river ran uphill instead of downhill as do most rivers, asked how water could run uphill. The teacher slammed his book shut, pounded his desk with his fist, strode over to Tom with his eyebrows twitching up and down, and is reported to have said, "Thomas Alva, you always ask entirely too many questions. You are addled." By now, Tom had begun to regard himself as a hopeless dunce, and his father had begun to have vague anxieties about his son's stupidity. Tom's mother, however, recognized the boy's talent for asking difficult and puzzling questions as a valuable one, and she held no high opinion of the school's methods and results. With his mother, young Tom found study easy and exciting.

Albert Einstein also suffered a great deal because of his proclivity for asking questions about things which puzzled him. His mother apparently loved and encouraged this tendency. His father was occasionally somewhat exhausted by it, but nonetheless accepted it and responded with liveliness and understanding. Young Einstein found no such response in the German schools that he attended, however, and he disliked school rather intensely until, at a later time, he found a school in Switzerland where his questions were respected. But at the Luitpold Gymnasium in Munich, teachers did not like him because he asked so many questions, and they sometimes thrashed him for this offense.

Insight into the reasons that this questioning characteristic makes a child difficult is reflected in the interview between Einstein and his science teacher on the day he became a school "dropout." The teacher asked young Einstein to remain after class and told him that he was a "bad" influence on the other pupils, causing them to lose respect for the teacher. The teacher had apparently compiled a list of the embarrassing questions Albert had asked. His list included such questions as: "Why can't we feel the earth move?" "What is space?" "What keeps the world from flying into pieces as it spins around?" The teacher confessed that he could not answer Einstein's questions and that no one else could. He then reported that it was the consensus of the other teachers in the school, as well, that young Einstein withdraw from the Gymnasium.

It is unfortunate that these teachers and the many others throughout history who have been tortured by the puzzling questions of their pupils could not have recognized this characteristic as a tremendously valuable one. Fundamental to any creative thinking is the ability to recognize missing gaps in knowledge and to recognize problems and defects. There is no reason that such questions should be so threatening to teachers and cause them to fear that they will lose the respect of their pupils.

Need to Meet Challenge and to Attempt Difficult Tasks

Another common creative need is to meet challenge and to attempt difficult and dangerous tasks (Torrance, 1968a). Outstanding creative achievement involves a successful step into the unknown, being different, testing known limits, attempting difficult jobs, making honest mistakes, and responding to challenge. One of the truly important factors in highly creative achievement is a strong tendency toward stress-seeking.

The tendency "to attempt difficult tasks," however, is not regarded as a very desirable one by teachers and parents who responded to my ideal pupil checklist. "Preference for complex tasks" ranks thirty-fifth among teachers in the United States and thirty-seventh among parents. Similar rankings are noted in all seven of the other countries studied. "Attempting difficult tasks" ranks ninteenth among teachers and twenty-second among parents in the United States, with only the German teachers giving it a rank among the top twelve characteristics. "Willingness to take risks" ranks thirty-sixth among both parents and teachers in the United States and holds a similar position in the other countries for which we have data.

The boyhoods of personages such as Edison, Einstein, Franklin, Byrd, and others are filled with accounts of their attempts to accomplish tasks which were too difficult for them. Usually they calculated the risks rather carefully, but all of them inevitably made mistakes or experienced dangers which placed them in the category of "difficult children."

Young Tom Edison, in his enthusiasm for studying lighter-than-air gases, incurred the displeasure of even his mother when his friend, Michael, at Tom's instigation, drank Seidlitz gas to make him float and subsequently became ill. On this occasion, Mrs. Edison made Tom go to bed without supper and told him that he would have to destroy all the bottles in his laboratory. She relented, however, in the matter of the destruction of his laboratory. During Tom's adolescence, he lost his railroad job after there was an explosion in the laboratory which he had on board the train.

As a boy, Benjamin toyed with danger when he devised a kite which would drag him along the water as he floated. But one time, the kite drew him backwards, dragging his head under water. He became so tired from hanging onto the kitestring that he might have been drowned had he been a less powerful swimmer. Franklin also fashioned a set of paddles for his hands and feet. He strapped them on with leather and used them in swimming. He was able to calculate the risk, however, and discarded them when they proved to be too heavy. It seems to be characteristic of highly creative people that they test carefully the limits of their abilities, the situation, and the materials and methods which they create.

Young Wilbur and Orville Wright were continually testing the limits with their box kites. The dangers of crashing and injuring themselves were forever obvious. On one occasion, Orville did crash into a tree while riding the kite. This miscalculation is said to have resulted in their desire to control the movement of the kite and thus in one of the breakthroughs which made mechanical flight possible.

At age ten, Richard Byrd wandered widely over the countryside, through the woods and into caves. One time, a nearby tree was struck by lightning, and a flash flood took out a bridge which he had to cross. Consequently, he arrived at home long after dark. Although Byrd's parents were anxious about his safety on this occasion, they later permitted him to take a trip around the world, even before he was graduated from high school. And so we see Byrd, and many others who have made outstanding creative contributions to mankind, learning during their early years the skills of testing the limits of their abilities, of testing the situation, and of testing their other resources—skills which were later to make them great. It seems to me that this need to test the limits is an important one, and that children should be taught the skills of testing the limits under alert and sensitive guidance.

Need to Give Oneself Completely to a Task

Another common creative need and one that many people have difficulty understanding is the need to give oneself completely to a task and to become fully absorbed in it. The creative child frequently becomes so preoccupied with his ideas and problems that he is inattentive to whatever is going on around him. Such individuals are frequently considered absentminded. Their parents and teachers find such behavior annoying and frequently forbid the particular activities which are so absorbing. Such a complaint is frequently made concerning the children who, we find, are most outstanding on tests of creative thinking. Some children, however, even become so preoccupied about a specific part of the test or about something outside the test that they do not perform well on the test.

It was this tendency to become absorbed in an interesting task that caused young Tom Edison to be considered a difficult child on his first day of school. As the writing lesson began, Tom was holding his sketch pad on his slate and was drawing a picture of the new "House in the Grove" which had attracted his attention on the way to school. As the teacher chanted, " 'Round and 'round. Crayon up!" Tom paid no attention. The teacher repeated, "Crayon up, Thomas Alva!" Tom was so absorbed with his drawing that he still did not hear. Suddenly, Tom sensed that the room was quiet, and he could feel the angry teacher coming toward him. The teacher snatched the paper out of Tom's hands, made him sit in the corner the remainder of the morning and into the lunch hour, and tore up the drawing.

Albert Einstein was fortunate in that his family understood his frequent absorption in thought and that they did not punish him. On one occasion, Albert had been thinking so hard that he had forgotten where he was. Some of the men thought the boy had been asleep but Albert declared that he was just thinking. His Uncle Jacob defended him, saying that he often caught the boy lost in thought. Albert's mother frequently worried because he would go for a walk in the rain and become so preoccupied with his ideas that it would never occur to him to put on his coat.

Need to Be Honest and to Search for the Truth

Honesty is the very essence of the creative personality. Perhaps unconsciously, however, we condition children through the home, school, church, and community to be less than honest. Certainly independence in judgment, courage in convictions, emotional sensitivity, intuition, and openness to experience are all important in creativity and are seriously impaired by subtle conditioning to dishonesty. Unfortunately, however, none of these characteristics is very highly valued by United States parents and teachers, if we can accept the results of our studies involving the ideal pupil checklist. Quite interestingly, independence in thinking is highly valued (ranking second among teachers and seventh among parents), but it is a somewhat different matter in the case of independence in judgment which ranks twenty-first among both teachers and parents. Genuine creative achievement requires that an individual be able to make independent judgment and to have the courage to stick to his conclusions and to work toward their achievement, even though he may be a minority of one at the beginning. Being courageous is valued even less than independent judgment among teachers (twenty-ninth), although it ranks eighteenth among parents. Emotional sensitivity ranks forty-seventh among both teachers and parents in the United States, and being intuitive ranks thirtieth among teachers and thirty-fourth among parents.

An incident from the early life of Albert Einstein will illustrate how a child's honesty may cause him to be considered difficult. Albert was sometimes ridiculed by his peers for being honest and was nicknamed "Honest John." One day, he was so absorbed in his dreams and thoughts that he failed to notice a group of passing soldiers. One of the officers asked the other boys who Albert was. They said, "Oh, that's 'Honest John.'" When asked to explain, the boys told the officer that "because Albert is not very bright, he always tells the truth, even if it gets him into trouble." The officer then called the boy over and taunted him for not playing soldier with the other boys. Albert explained that he did not want to play soldier and that he was not going to be a soldier. This enraged the officer who made the boy tell him where he lived. Albert was told by both the officer and his parents that he would have to be a soldier. This frightening incident apparently gave him an intense desire to escape from Germany.

Need to Be Different, to Be an Individual

In some ways, one of the most fundamental creative needs is to be different, to be an individual, to be oneself. This is not for the sake of being different, but because the creative person has to be different in order to attain his potentialities. Rarely, however, do we respect the child's need to be an individual. We are more concerned about "appearing to be" than about "being." Even when one is different in ways which are defined as socially desirable, he finds himself under pressure. He may work too hard and learn more than he should. He may be too honest, too courageous, too altruistic, or too affectionate. He may be too adventurous, too curious, or too determined. Parents do not want their children to be considered different or peculiar, and teachers endeavor to make children conform to behavioral norms or become socially well-adjusted. Being different does not seem to bother young children, but year by year, they become increasingly more afraid of being themselves.

The awesomeness of being different is well-understood by most children by the time they reach the fourth grade. Children have told me this in many ways. Its impact became clearest when we asked children to write imaginative stories about animals or people with some divergent characteristics. Most revealing were the stories about the flying monkey. In the stories written by the children, the parents of the flying monkey are upset when they learn that their child is a flying monkey. They may send him to another part of the jungle; they do not want him and reject him. They may think that he is mentally ill and take him to a doctor. Or, the mother may have the father give him a "good talking to" and tell him that the other animals will think that he is "crazy in the head," if he continues to fly. They may tell the flying monkey that others will be afraid of him or that he will have no friends. They may teach him how to hide his wings or camouflage them so that others will not know that he can fly. Or, they may cut off his wings. They warn him of all kinds of punishment and destruction. It is always the good little monkey who gives up his flying and other peculiar behavior. Even when the monkey's flying ability is used for the good of others, such as obtaining the bananas at the top of the tree for the other monkeys, he may be ridiculed and punished for being different.

Developing Respect for Children's Creative Needs

Recognizing that in the ordinary course of events, teachers and parents have rarely shown very much respect for the creative needs of children, I have devoted a great deal of thought to the problem of finding ways in which we might develop and manifest greater respect for these needs.

Early in our investigations, I became convinced that we could best respect creative needs and serve the purposes of creative growth in the classroom by respecting the questions that children ask, by respecting the ideas that they present for consideration, by showing them that their ideas have value, by encouraging opportunities for practice and experimentation without evaluation and grading, and by encouraging and giving credit for self-initiated learning and thinking. We called these principles for rewarding creative behavior, and we made them the basis for some of our teachers' manuals and in-service education programs.

While some educators and psychologists have attacked these "principles" as being unvalidated hypotheses, others have criticized them as being nothing more than "self-evident truisms and annoyingly pat exhortations." I must admit that my observations of classroom teaching made these ideas seem obvious, but I rarely found teachers applying them. Rather, I found teachers violating them. If these principles were self-evident truisms, I was convinced that few teachers acted as though they really believed them. Therefore, I maintained that the application of these simple ideas, such as being respectful of children's ideas and questions, could be a very powerful force in encouraging the development of potential as well as the development of the new type of human being about which we are concerned.

We asked teachers, ones who had participated in in-service education groups and who had used our manuals, to describe experiences in which they had applied these principles. It was clear from these highly selective data that many teachers did not understand and accept these ideas, but that those who applied them with fidelity, produced creative growth.

An Exercise

I have summarized the results of the study just cited in *Rewarding Creative Behavior* (Torrance, 1965a), and I could summarize them here. But I believe you would find out far more if you would carry out one of the following exercises or projects.

If you are teaching or practice teaching, try to enlist some of your colleagues in a kind of workshop on developing skills of being respectful of unusual questions and ideas. If you cannot get your colleagues to cooperate, you can carry it out by yourself.

I propose that you do the following things in these workshops:

1. Think about what it really means to be respectful of the questions and ideas of children. Really think! Dig deep!
2. Try deliberately to be respectful of the questions and ideas of your pupils.
3. Write detailed descriptions of one incident in which you tried to be respectful of an unusual and vexing question, and one incident in which you tried to be respectful of an original idea presented by a pupil.
4. Discuss your descriptions with one another, trying to decide how well each of you succeeded in being respectful of the pupil's questions and ideas—not just appearing to be respectful. Then try to produce a variety of other possible ways by which each of you could have been more genuinely respectful, thereby encouraging increased creativity and learning.

In writing your descriptions of the incidents in which you tried to be respectful of a pupil's questions and/or ideas, the following questions might be used as a guide:

1. What was the question (idea)? Who asked (expressed) it? What were the general conditions under which it was asked (proposed)?
2. What was your own immediate reaction?
3. What was the immediate reaction of the class?
4. In what way was respect shown for the question (idea)?
5. What, if any, were the observable effects (immediate and/or long range)?

If you are not teaching or practice teaching, use the material in Appendix B as the basis for a similar exercise. First, try to predict the possible outcomes of the incidents described. Then, try to empathize, first with the teacher and then with the pupil. Was genuine respect shown by the teacher? What kept the teacher from showing genuine respect for the pupil's question or idea? Why do you think the teacher thought he was being respectful of the question or idea? (You will find other such incidents described in *Rewarding Creative Behavior*.)

3

Knowing the Learner

To respond creatively to a pupil, to enter into a creative relationship with him, to be able to empathize with him, and to recognize and acknowledge his potentialities, a teacher must genuinely know him. Seldom do teachers stop to think what it means to know a child. Following a recent laboratory experience in a graduate course on the learning problems of disadvantaged children, several experienced teachers wrote, "I have taught many disadvantaged children, but I have never known one before." After the first day of the laboratory experience, one teacher reported, "That was the longest thirty minutes of my life. I thought I would die. I look with horror to three weeks of this workshop." Fortunately, however, this teacher, too, came to know the child to whom she had been assigned and found real excitement in the relationship.

Instead of presenting a full psychological rationale concerning the importance of knowing pupils and suggesting a host of ideas for knowing children and adolescents, I would like to invite you to embark upon an adventure. Select some common object in your environment—a tree, a rock, a piece of wood, a stick—almost anything. Spend the next thirty minutes in deliberate, intense effort to know this object. Use every method you can think of to get to know this object without damaging it. Feel it, smell it, listen to it, experiment with it, imagine yourself in its place—whatever you can think of. Write down each awareness that comes to you. Be receptive but make it an active thing. Do not stop too early! Just when you think you have exhausted every possibility of knowing your object, you will think of a flood of other ideas, more exciting ones than ever. Remember, however, it does take effort!

After you have exhausted every way you can think of for knowing your object, reflect upon the experience. What ways did you use in getting to know your object? What resources did you find that you had for knowing the object? What was there about your attitudes, personality, or learning style that helped or hindered you? What can you do about these matters?

I have used this exercise a dozen or more times with classes and workshops varying in size from ten to over 200, and it has always been an exciting experience for both the group and me. I know a high school physics teacher who uses an exercise very similar to this. He gives each of his pupils a ball bearing. When he gives these ball bearings to his pupils, he checks the fact that they cannot distinguish one from another. He encourages them to carry the ball bearings with them at all times and to get to know them. After a couple of weeks, he has the pupils pile the ball bearings on his desk. He then mixes them up and asks the pupils to come to his desk to pick out their own ball bearings. Usually, all of them can do this successfully. The teacher has, prior to experiments, worked out a way of marking the ball bearing so that the identifying symbols are invisible to the pupils but can be made evident by chemical and magnification processes.

In a workshop of approximately 100 Oregon teachers, I conducted an exercise in knowing by using small pieces of wood. The first hour one morning was devoted to the problem of developing ideas, concepts, and procedures for knowing children through the analogy of "knowing a piece of wood." Following this one-hour experience and a twenty-minute coffee break, I asked the workshop participants to develop a set of guidelines for knowing children and adolescents. The following instructions were given:

> On the basis of our laboratory experience with the piece of wood, formulate a set of guides for getting to know children and young people, their qualities, and their potentialities. Do not be preoccupied with specific "bits" of information about the person but focus on ways of "knowing."

The following is a sample of the ideas formulated, arranged in such a way as to provide a kind of composite picture of the ideas produced. They may help you see more in your experience.

A. IDEAS RELEVANT TO AN AWARENESS OF THE PERSON'S INDIVIDUALITY

1. Remember that potentialities have to be looked for and that this takes effort.
2. Try to discover something unique about each child or young person.
3. Expect him to be different.
4. Identify him by name as early as possible.
5. Remember that children come in many different shapes, sizes, colors. Each has his own personality that needs to be differentiated.

6. Remember that each has his own pattern of learning and that it is important to "tune in to it" or become aware of it.
7. Accept him as he is. Every child and young person has interesting, exciting, and valuable qualities.
8. Observe the environmental effects on him; know the environmental background.
9. Be aware of the previous injuries or experiences that have shaped his way of thinking, acting, and feeling.
10. Be familiar with his past record, achievement, discipline, health, etc.
11. Learn something of his family relationships ("chip off old block").
12. Know what the normal pattern is and compare to see how his pattern differs from it.
13. Remember that we never learn all there is to know about a person.

B. IDEAS INVOLVING HEIGHTENED SENSORY EXPERIENCE

14. Look him over.
15. Focus your attention directly on him.
16. A child's physical qualities are one way of knowing him.
17. Use all your senses of "knowing"—stretching them to the utmost.
18. Be a good listener—really hear and consider what he says.
19. Weigh and test.
20. Look at, listen to, react to him from *all* angles.
21. Observe in various kinds of light (in as many situations as possible). Bright lights bring out some characteristics, while shade brings out others.
22. Observe the child first as an isolated individual, and then his reaction to his environment, the reactions of others to him, and his behavior in different situations.
23. Test the depth and genuineness of his observable (surface) characteristics. What you might assume to be sham or pretense may be genuine.
24. Observe what he does when left alone.
25. Empathize. Try to imagine how he experiences things.
26. Construct fantasies or dream castles about what he could become.
27. Observe cleanliness or lack of cleanliness. What appears to be uncleanliness may only be stains.
28. Go below the surface appearance to find the real child.
29. See him from all sides and positions.
30. Notice physical differences so as to distinguish one pupil from another as early as possible.
31. Photograph him engaged in various kinds of activities. Record his voice.

32. Observe whether he is relaxed or tense.
33. Look, look, look, and then look again.

C. Extension of Sensing through Experimentation

34. Encourage him to go further than he thinks he can, to test his limits.
35. Find his most obvious assets, put them to use, and see what others emerge.
36. Do not be afraid to challenge a child or a young person to his limits occasionally, even to the frustration point.
37. Provide materials for manipulation, give opportunities for their use, and see what potentialities emerge.
38. Set up a variety of situations where he may work alone, with one, with a committee, and with a structured class, and observe changes in behavior.
39. Observe his response to different environmental factors.
40. Alter the classroom structure.
41. Give him an interest inventory of some kind.
42. Challenge him with a variety of types of assignments and note the results.
43. Use him for an important purpose or goal and observe what new potentialities this brings out.
44. Observe him under stress, when he is angry, etc.
45. Observe what he chooses to do when he is alone.
46. Give him opportunities to pursue his hobbies or strong interests as a way of bringing out some of his best abilities and strongest motivations.
47. Observe changes or lack of change (stability) under different conditions.
48. Keep changing the conditions. Give different activities to bring out new potentialities that don't just happen to come out.
49. Observe how he responds and to what he responds.
50. Let him act independently.
51. Give him a chance to express himself.
52. Experiment and evaluate; observe what new qualities come out under various conditions.
53. Use a variety of ways of testing them.
54. Develop or enhance one potentiality and see what others come out.
55. Joke with him.
56. Needle him.
57. Remember that every child and young person has infinite potentialities, and there is no end to them if we are open, and if we exert effort.

58. Observe him under stress and competition.
59. Synthesize test scores and other data into a coherent, meaningful picture.

D. Extending Awareness by Recording, Predicting, and Checking Predictions

60. After making observations, predict how the child or young person will perform (behave, achieve, react, respond) in various situations; how he will meet predictable stresses, etc.
61. Have him react to certain objects, and predict his reaction.
62. Withhold final judgment. Keep open to changes and unseen potentialities.
63. List observable characteristics. Write down predictions and keep a record of their outcome.
64. Record observations from time to time, over a span of time. Observe trends.
65. When you combine his potentialities with someone else's, what new qualities emerge?
66. Examine performance data, if available. Study growth trends.

E. Extending Awareness through Interpersonal Reaction

67. Find ways of rearranging children for greater interaction.
68. Allow children to work in teams, and listen and observe to see what unexpected qualities are manifested.
69. Observe what talents, interests, or motivations emerge in role playing, playground activities, lunchroom interaction, fantasy activities, etc.
70. Observe the child's behavior in different combinations of other pupils.
71. Ask other people about him; find out how others see him.
72. Use sociograms and other peer ratings, interaction information, etc.
73. Observe how he interacts with his peers in the classroom.
74. Compare him with others his age, sex, etc.
75. Notice his moods and reactions day after day; observe how his presence or absence affects others.

F. Using Self in Interaction Process

76. Remember that warmth of personality is felt only by contact, association, etc.
77. Touch him.
78. Hold him.
79. Caress him.
80. Converse with the child or young person individually.

81. Act as a responsive environment.
82. Be available, always take time to listen, and look for potentialities.
83. Be really interested; really care.
84. Try to get to know him well enough to discover what "warms" or "sparks" him.
85. Love him.
86. Enjoy him.
87. Work and play along with him; co-experience, co-learn.

G. Through Heightened Consciousness

88. Become aware of your own biases—potentialities you tend either to see or to ignore.
89. Instead of forcing the child into your mold, think of ways of helping him develop as he is, using his own best potentialities.
90. Become aware of the child or young person's effect on you emotionally.
91. Remember that no child or young person is dull or uninteresting; it takes time and quiet effort to find the qualities that make him unique.
92. A person's potentialities are many-sided; sometimes we see only one dominant quality and miss all the others.
93. Do not let a label blind you to what the child really is and can become. The label may sometimes be incorrect or inappropriate.
94. Know what biases and limitations for awareness keep you from understanding a child or young person.
95. Reflect about the child and your own feelings about him.
96. Take time out to become aware of his potentialities.
97. Keep open to the child's developmental and behavioral pattern.
98. Seek to know the child intimately and intuitively.
99. After making observations, let the processes of incubation operate.
100. Differentiate the similarities and differences between you and him; do not assume that he responds as you do in all respects.

4

Building Creative Skills

A large proportion of unsuccessful teaching is caused by the teacher's failure to build upon the necessary component or foundation skills that the learner has already acquired. People do not learn when tasks are either too easy or too difficult. They learn best those things that are challenging—things that require effort but which can be mastered by them.

One of the oldest controversies regarding the nature of human learning and development is concerned with the continuity-discontinuity question. The idea that human learning and development are not and, indeed, should not be continuous but should move in great beats and surges dates back to very ancient times. In my estimation, this is still the prevailing notion among teachers.

Pestalozzi and Froebel believed that it is healthy and natural for development to be continuous, and they worked at ways of developing sequences of activities and kinds of guided experiences that would increase the chances of this continuity. These concerns are clearly manifested in Pestalozzi's *How Gertrude Teaches Her Children* (1894) and Froebel's *Mother's Songs, Games, and Stories* (1891). Both of these books were designed for use by mothers so that this continuity could be accomplished from infancy onward. As an example, Pestalozzi cautioned that mothers should arrange experiences according to graduated steps of knowledge so that every new idea would be only a small, almost imperceptible addition to earlier knowledge which was already deeply impressed and unforgettable. He also advised that the simple should be made perfect before going on to the complex.

Froebel thought that his book for mothers should also be known by kindergarten teachers so that they could continue the hometraining and not interrupt the child's stages of development. He stressed the point that school should bring new scenes, fresh acquaintances, and a general widening of the child's sphere, but that continuity would "make

31

the child feel at home" and facilitate learning. Thus, he recommended that the finger and arm activities, as well as other activities used in guiding learning, be continued by kindergarten teachers until such activities are replaced by other methods of guidance better suited to the child's mental and physical development. Connectedness is a major theme in Froebel's methods. His methods for guiding learning were designed to keep form, language, and number closely connected. The drawings in his book for mothers illustrate his penchant for connectedness. For example, in one illustration to teach the concept of "wind," he has the weather-cock or vane turning, trees with their leaves and branches blowing, a flag flying in the wind, a flying kite, the mother's and the children's hair blowing, laundry blowing on the clothesline, and the like. Froebel instructed the mothers to let their children's hands carry out the movements of the wind and of the things that the wind is moving. He offers this verse:

> As the cock, up on the Tower,
>   Turns in wind and storm and shower,
> Baby can bend his hand and learn
> To get joy at every turn. (Froebel, 1891, p. 17)

Shirreff, championing Froebel's educational principles in the American journal, *Education,* in 1881, criticized educational systems that "seek to impose a new nature, as it were, upon the child, to cultivate one set of faculties to the neglect of others, to impose knowledge of a certain kind, instead of aiding the newly awakened intelligence" (p. 425). He asserted that all such systems are false and can never rightly educate.

In France, Alfred Binet (1909) was keenly aware of the discontinuities in education there and sought to develop instructional procedures that would reduce the discontinuities. He believed that, at the time they first came to school, children had already developed some powerful skills for learning and that the school should graft education onto these already developed skills. In this way, the teacher could benefit from the start already made by nature. He believed that nature would furnish the activity and that teachers need intervene only to guide or direct it. He recognized that children entered school with such learning skills as manipulating objects, moving them about, changing them to construct others, questioning, singing, drawing, storytelling, and inventing.

Montessori's (1964) methods also emphasized both the continuity among the various aspects of the curriculum and among the various aspects of personality. Her methods also recognized the importance of continuity in the sense of not interrupting children absorbed in a learning task to rush them to a different learning task, previously scheduled. She wrote: "He who interrupts the children in their occupations in order to make them to learn some predetermined thing; he who makes them cease the study of arithmetic to pass on to that of geography and the like, thinking it is important to direct their culture, confuses the means with the end and destroys the man for a vanity" (p. 180).

Curiosity, the instinct of play, the instinct to manipulate, and the like have been suggested as natural guides to learning. Educational innovators such as Pestalozzi, Froebel, Binet, Montessori, and others made use of these forces but recognized clearly that curiosity, playfulness, and manipulativeness, unguided, cannot be depended upon to bring about learning. As Barnard pointed out regarding the modeling instinct, "Education must supply the material and guidance necessary for the development, must convert the aimless touching and fumbling into systematic construction, and direct the instinct into a channel of useful activity . . ." (Barnard, 1879, p. 173).

Educators and psychiatrists have long recognized that the periods of greatest discontinuity in development are accompanied by sharp increases in mental, emotional, and physical disturbances. While a majority of them have apparently assumed that those discontinuities are healthy and should be preserved, a small minority have urged that these discontinuities be reduced, either by some administrative arrangement, or through some change in the degree and type of guidance offered.

In my own studies of the discontinuities in creative development (Torrance, 1962, 1963, 1967a), the culture or man-made nature of these discontinuities has become apparent. And yet it is also clear that the intervention of the teacher and of instructional materials is so powerful that these discontinuities can be reduced or practically eliminated (Torrance and Gupta, 1964). The issues inherent in the continuity concept are especially relevant to such current issues as the ungraded school, the reorganization of the school day into larger blocks of time, team teaching, and the like.

Susceptibility of Mental Abilities to Development

Educational thinkers who have contributed to the development of the concept, guided learning, have generally held that mental abilities are susceptible to development through educational experiences. Through the years, investigators have presented empirical data to challenge the concept of fixed intelligence. Despite this, the view that intelligence is a capacity fixed once and for all by genetic inheritance is widespread even today. A great deal of empirical evidence has seemed, at first glance, to support the idea of fixed intelligence. Recently, however, Hunt (1961, 1968) proposed alternative explanations, and he summarized evidence that undermines this idea. Hunt also cited studies showing that, out of groups of people tested at some earlier age, those who complete the most schooling show the greatest increases and fewest decreases in I.Q.

Alfred Binet (1909) spoke out quite strongly against the prevailing prejudice of his day toward the "educability of intelligence." He remarked that the familiar proverb, "When one is stupid, it is for a long time," seemed to be taken literally by teachers. He reproached the predominant methods of education of his day, methods which brought into play almost exclusively the memory abilities and which reduced the learner to a condition of passivity. Like many recent observers of classroom behavior, Binet observed in French schools that pupils were rarely called upon to judge anything, reflect upon anything, or produce anything. They needed only to retain and reproduce. The ideal pupil recited without making a mistake, and the goal of the teacher was to make the pupil's memory function, to see that he knew what was in the textbook, and to see that he could repeat it cleverly at the examination. Binet argued that, for the pupil, the result of these deplorable practices was a lack of curiosity, a tendency to seek truth solely in the book, an indifference to his environment, a naive belief in the omnipotence of formulas, lack of adaptation to contemporary life, and a routine mind that is "sadly out of place in an epoch when society evolves with infernal speed."

Binet (1909) believed that the child should be taught to produce and to test ideas on his own, to act spontaneously, to judge for himself, to participate in the life about him, to explain what he sees, to defend his own ideas, to practice making decisions, to learn how to orient himself, to plan his days, to imagine, to invent, to live on his own account, and to feel at once the excellence and the responsibility of free action. From the studies available in the experimental psychology of his day, Binet believed that it had been demonstrated beyond a doubt that every thought and mental function is susceptible to development. He maintained that every time anyone has taken the trouble to repeat methodically any type of work that has had measurable effects, the results follow a characteristic curve of learning.

In recent years, there has been a variety of studies to determine whether or not the productive thinking abilities are susceptible to improvement through educational experiences. In almost all cases, the results have been positive (Parnes and Meadow, 1959, 1960; Samson, 1965; Torrance, 1963, 1965a). Binet's hypotheses, built on the theories of Rousseau, Spencer, and Froebel, and on the experimental psychology of his day, continue to be supported in our own day, at least so far as I am able to interpret the data. Apparently, the various mental functions, especially those involved in productive thinking, are like skills and thus require opportunity for guided practice in order to develop to any high degree (Bartlett, 1958; Singer, 1964). This seems to be as true of imagination and fantasy as of logical reasoning and judgment.

As our ability to differentiate and assess different kinds of mental functioning has improved, we are beginning to understand some of the puzzling findings of the past in educational research. For example, we need no longer be puzzled by McConnell's finding (1934) that mental age as measured by an intelligence test is more highly related to achievement in second grade arithmetic when taught by authoritative identification than when taught by the methods of discovery. Hutchinson (1963), in a study involving learning in junior high school social studies, also found that, under traditional authoritarian teaching, there is a statistically significant positive correlation between mental age and achievement but not between measures of divergent thinking and achievement. In experimental conditions offering considerable opportunities for learning in creative ways, the reverse was true.

In a study involving fifth grade children using programmed instruction in language arts, Gotkin and Massa (1963) found significant negative relationships between measures of divergent thinking and achievement. Stolurow (1964) found higher positive correlations between measures of originality and achievement than between mental age and achievement with programmed materials in mathematics and statistics. The difference was that Gotkin and Massa used materials that permitted only tiny mental leaps and gave little opportunity for making, identifying, and correcting errors, while Stolurow's materials emphasized a troubleshooting or hypothesizing approach that builds specific but multiple associations to a stimulus.

MacDonald and Raths (1964) found that highly creative or divergent thinking children are more productive on frustrating tasks than are less creative children. Furthermore, the highly creative children enjoy such tasks more than their less creative peers do. The least creative children are less productive in open tasks, and the most creative ones react less favorably to closed tasks. Consequently, pupils of varying levels of creative or divergent thinking ability react differently to different kinds of curriculum tasks and are possibly best taught by varying procedures.

Sequences of Activities

Common to all who have made signal contributions to the development of the concept, "guided learning," has been the formulation of some scheme for arranging sequences of activities—from easy to difficult, from simple to complex, from concrete to abstract, from top to bottom and vice versa, from beginning to end of a process, and the like. In some schemes, activities have been arranged to conform to a conceptualization or model of the problem-solving process. Some of the schemes offered by the leading thinkers will be summarized here.

Pestalozzi (1894) suggested that learning activities be arranged in sequences in accordance with the laws for the development of the human mind. These laws, as formulated by him, are as follows:

1. Classify observations and complete the simple before proceeding to the complex.
2. Bring all things essentially related to one another to that connection in your mind which they have in nature. Subordinate all unessential things to the essential in your idea.
3. Strengthen and make clear the impressions of important objects by bringing them nearer to you and letting them affect you through the senses.
4. Regard all the effects of natural law as absolutely necessary, and recognize in this necessity the result of her power by which nature unites together the apparently heterogeneous elements of her materials for the achievement of her end.
5. But the richness of its charm (art) and the variety of its free play cause physical necessity, or natural law, to bear the impress of freedom and independence.

According to him, the first instruction should be sounds (spoken, sung, etc.), followed by form, and then by other sense impressions.

Herbart (Broudy, 1963) developed a teaching method that served as a guide for ordering sequences of learning activities. His followers have changed the labels of his steps *from* (1) clearness, (2) association, (3) systematization, and (4) method, *to* (1) preparation, (2) presentation, (3) association, (4) systematization, and (5) application. The preparation step has two aspects, the motivational and the cognitive.

Froebel's concepts concerning the arrangement of learning tasks into sequences are illustrated in his list of thirteen gifts and eleven occupations and in the exercises in his book for mothers (Bowen, 1906; Barnard, 1879; Froebel, 1891, 1904).

The first gift consisted of six worsted balls, each having one of the colors of the rainbow, with strings attached. The ball was chosen as the first gift because it is the simplest and most complete ground form. It is the first plaything that a mother gives her child; it is light and soft; it can easily be taken hold of; and it fascinates because of its tendency to constant motion. Froebel believed that the balls satisfied the child's unconscious need for wholeness—to contemplate, grasp, and possess a whole. He offered a variety of suggestions for guiding learning using the balls as the object. The balls represent the elements of form, color, motion, and size; observations and comparisons can be made of these elements. The balls also provide such exercises as grasping, catching, moving on strings to educate the eye in fixing a point, games in the air to excite healthy action of the entire body and to awaken grace in all movements, and gymnastics (hopping when the ball hops, etc.). He found that the balls were suitable for children in the nursery up to three years of age and for kindergarten children who had not had experience with balls. A variety of games was also suggested for using the ball for learning purposes.

The other gifts, to be used for experimentation to find out what could be done with them, were as follows:

2. Sphere, cylinder, and cube (of wood—hard, smooth, heavy, and resonant);
3. A box containing a cube subdivided by three cuttings into eight cubes, each one representing the large cube on a smaller scale;
4. A cube divided into eight blocks, each two inches long, one inch wide, and one-half inch high;
5. A cube divided into twenty-seven equal cubes;
6. A cube divided into twenty-seven oblongs of the same size as in the fourth gift;
7. The wood tables, usually made of two colors, and in two shapes;
8. The connected slat which represents the embodied edge of the whole square, triangle, pentagon, etc. (Ten slats, each four inches long and one-half inch wide, riveted together at the ends so that they can be folded or unfolded to give different forms);
9. The disconnected slat or slat interlacing (wooden slats of varying lengths, widths, and textures, about ten inches long and two-fifths of an inch wide, secured in bundles of ten or twelve);
10. Sticks for stick laying (representation of the line or edge of a surface);
11. Wire rings and half-circles of three different sizes ranging from one to two inches in diameter, for ring laying;
12. The thread game (a thread in which the ends are joined, made of cotton);
13. The point, the embodied corner of the cube, peas or lentils.

After the gifts came the occupations, as follows:

14. Perforating (pricking)—using a needle mounted in a wooden handle, the child can prick out pictures on white paper mounted over a perforating cushion;

15. Sewing (embroidery) pictures on cardboard;
16. Net-work drawing—drawing-books containing ruled pages;
17. Painting (water colors, brushes, and a book containing pictures arranged progressively);
18. Mat-plaiting, weaving, braiding;
19. Paper interlacing (intertwining);
20. Paper folding (square, rectangular, and triangular pieces);
21. Paper cutting, paper mounting, and silhouetting;
22. Peas or cork work;
23. Cardboard work;
24. Modeling (modeling wax and molding knife).

Binet (1909) apparently made most of his decisions about arranging activities into sequences according to the difficulty principle, "the greatest principle of pedagogy," in his opinion. He held that it was necessary to proceed from the easy to the difficult and that the transgression of this principle was almost universal and gave rise to the most deplorable errors on the part of even the most intelligent teachers. He believed that a little difficulty is a good thing and is a stimulus to a good pupil, but too great difficulty is overwhelming and has rather serious consequences, resulting in the disorganization of intelligence.

Parker (Cremin, 1961) borrowed quite heavily from Pestalozzi, Froebel, and Herbart and produced a synthesis that is usually regarded as marking a transition from early American transcendentalism to a newer scientific pedagogy, and from dependence on European formulations to a more indigenous effort. Parker (Boraas, 1922, p. 165) summarized the sequencing of activities in reflective thinking as follows:

1. *Define* the problem at issue and keep it clearly in mind.
2. *Recall* as many related ideas as possible by analyzing the situation and formulating definite hypotheses, and by recalling general rules and principles that may apply.
3. *Evaluate* carefully each suggestion by maintaining an attitude of unbiased, suspended judgment or conclusion, by criticizing each suggestion, by being systematic in selecting and rejecting suggestions, and by verifying conclusions.
4. *Organize* material so as to aid in the process of thinking by "taking stock" from time to time . . . using methods of tabulation and graphic expression, and expressing concisely the tentative conclusions reached from time to time during the inquiry.

It will be noted that this process is quite similar to the creative problem-solving process as formulated by Osborn (1963), Parnes (1967), Guilford (1966), and others. Guilford's model is one of the most elaborate of these models and may prove to be the most useful one thus far offered.

Tentative Hierarchy of Creative Skills: An Example

Until now, there has been little serious concern about identifying any kind of hierarchy of creative thinking skills that might be taught children. I am in the process of attempting to formulate and help implement a hierarchy of creative thinking skills to be built into a series of reading books prepared especially for disadvantaged children. It is geared to the creativity strand in the Ginn Reading 360 Program. Although the purpose of this formulation is limited, I believe that most aspects of it can be generalized to almost all other types of school learning. Thus far, I have formulated only the first six levels, but the formulation is sketched here for its suggestive value in furthering the development of some guiding principles for arranging sequences of activities involving the creative thinking abilities.

LEVEL 1

1. *The child will be able to produce new combinations through manipulation.*

Perhaps the most fundamental learning skill that the child brings with him to school, whether at age four, five, or six, is the manipulation of objects. Reading programs can build upon this learning skill by providing the guidance necessary to make these manipulative behaviors produce meaningful relationships greater than chance and to make certain relationships become meaningful ones.

Manipulation of *shapes* (lines, angles, triangles, circles, squares, rectangles, and finally, irregular shapes) can be used to discover and discriminate the alphabet and other meaningful symbols (pictures of the human face, human body, objects in the environment, etc.).

Manipulation of *sounds* can be used to develop auditory discriminations necessary for reading. At this level, the emphasis might be on producing animal sounds, developing a language of sound (long-short, slow-fast, heavy-light, etc.), and combining the elements of this language into the communication of feelings, actions, and so forth.

Manipulation of *colors* can be used in a gross way to lay the foundation for color discrimination and to interpret (read) the meaning in color. At this stage, manipulation might be limited to mixing the primary colors and might be implemented by something similar to Brown's (1958) *Color Kittens.*

Manipulation of *story characters, people, toys, and the like* through creative dramatics, puppet play, and so on can be used to lay the groundwork for story making, story reading, and so forth.

At the most fundamental level, simple manipulations of low-level complexity and natural trial-and-error manipulations should be emphasized. At the next level, more deliberate and complex manipulations can be stressed. Even at this most fundamental level, however, some emphasis can be made on helping the child give and get meaning from the combinations produced through manipulation.

2. *The child will be able to see and produce many possible combinations or new relationships.*

This second-level skill should be built deliberately and systematically upon the skills described in 1 above. In each area (shapes, sounds, etc.), children can be encouraged to apply creative thinking encouragers, such as: what all can be added, what will happen if you add   to   ? what can be subtracted, what will happen if you subtract   from   ? what will happen if you cut   into two parts? what will happen if you place this shape in the place of that one? and so forth. (See Osborn's principles for producing multiple alternatives in *Applied Imagination,* New York: Charles Scribner's Sons, 1963.)

Examples of children's literary materials that illustrate these principles in regard to the manipulation of shapes are:

EMBERLEY, ED. *The Wing on a Flea.* Boston: Little, Brown & Co., 1961.
UNGERER, TOMI. *Snail, Where Are You?* New York: Harper & Row, 1962.
WOLFF, JANET. *Let's Imagine Thinking Up Things.* New York: E. P. Dutton & Co., 1961.

Examples of children's literary materials that emphasize the production of multiple possibilities relevant to sounds are:

EMBERLEY, ED. *Cock a Doodle Doo: A Book of Sounds.* Boston: Little, Brown & Co., 1964.
TORRANCE, E. P. and PANSY. "Softest, Shortest, Slowest, Smallest . . ." *Music for Primaries,* 1969, 3(2), 22-24. (Also others in this same series.)
WOLFF, JANET. *Let's Imagine Sounds.* New York: E. P. Dutton & Co., 1962.

Children's literary materials on the manipulation of color to produce many possibilities are rather rare. The technique used in *Color Kittens* can be extended. The style and vocabulary of Mary O'Neill's *Hailstones and Halibut Bones* (1961) is somewhat difficult for children at this stage of development, but the technique of producing multiple associations to color can be used at least as early as age five. Joan W. Anglund's *What Color Is Love?* (1966) might also be useful.

At this level, possible combinations of people and animals might be limited to the manipulation of people and animals in settings or places. Examples of literary materials that might serve this purpose are:

BERENSTAIN, JANICE and STANLEY. *Inside, Outside, Upside Down.* New York: Random House, 1968.
WOLFF, JANET. *Let's Imagine Being Places.* New York: E. P. Dutton & Co., 1961.

Some of the *Just Imagine* series being developed by Elizabeth Kennedy and me also illustrate seeing possibilities of people in places. For example, one of them encourages children to imagine that on certain days they would play with the animals in the cages at the zoo. They then reenact, in creative dramatic fashion, the imaginary adventures they had when they entered the various cages at the zoo; this is followed by drawing pictures of their visit to the animal cages.

The dramatic and puppetry technique known as "Magic Net" may be used to develop skill in producing multiple combinations of people and animals in places (see Chapter 1). Literary material could be created to illustrate the technique and to orient children to its use. In brief, children given the "Magic Net" are turned into whatever characters they want to play. Directions are given by the Magic Storyteller who is given a special "Magic Net." The storyteller places the characters in various settings and situations, and the actors fulfill the story through mime technique.

3. *The child will be able to identify missing elements in pictures, shapes, letters, and so forth at a very gross level.*

Literary materials with missing elements could be created. Fine details should be avoided; only gross elements should be involved. Materials might involve objects cut into two parts, major elements omitted from pictures, gross discrepancies in pictures, one object behind another object, elements missing from letters of the alphabet, and the like. Also at a gross level, children might be encouraged to complete incomplete figures as in Task 2 of the *Torrance Tests of Creative Thinking* (1966). The drawings should be larger than the ones in the test booklet.

LEVEL 2

1. *The child will be able to produce increasingly more complex new combinations through manipulation, and move to more deliberate experimentation.*

At this stage, it should be possible to move the child to a stage of representing a structure at two or more levels of abstraction—on paper through a drawing, and concrete through the construction of a model.

Lego construction materials are good for this purpose. The children can be directed first to draw something—a castle, a dream house, a park, an airplane, an animal cage in a zoo, and so on. Then they can construct the object they have planned and drawn. They can also construct such things as the letters of the alphabet, numerals, and other symbols.

2. *The child will be able to see and produce increasingly larger numbers of possibilities in combining symbols, objects, numerals, people, places, and so forth.*

At this level, the child should be ready to move ahead to more varied shapes, sounds, and the like. There should be more emphasis on interpersonal combinations in different places, and on the consequences of these combinations. An interesting model which delights children of this age is *Tell a Tall Tale* by Kent Salisbury (1966). In this book, two characters, two places, and two consequences can be manipulated into hundreds of combinations. The idea itself is in "public domain" and has been used by storytellers for all ages. Original materials to achieve the objectives at this stage could readily be created.

3. *The child will increase his verbal fluency by naming new combinations of shapes, sounds, movements, animals, people, and so forth at a simple level.*

At first, it would probably be desirable to stick with rather simple and highly meaningful combinations and later to move to more fantastic ones. Exercises could involve the children in thinking of what certain shapes, sounds, movements, photographs, and the like remind them— what they could be.

4. *The child will be able to make simple syntheses by giving titles or labels to pictures, stories, songs, poems, creative dances, puppet plays, complex wood sculptures, and so on.*

Synthesis is one of the higher mental processes and must develop gradually. Generally, training is given in analysis but not in synthesis. Simple training in synthesizing should lay the groundwork for reading, especially in making use of titles, pictures, and the like.

5. *The child will improve his skills in asking questions about missing elements in objects, pictures, and so forth.*

At the time children enter school, they have begun to develop skills in asking questions to find out. In school, however, they are frequently given no opportunity to ask questions, and they fail to continue this development. Reading materials should be developed to encourage continuity of development of these skills. However, the teacher should not be discouraged if, at first, the children seem to hold fast to a particular kind of question such as the "why" question. Strange objects, pictures, and stories are good stimulus materials for exercises in developing question-asking skills about missing elements.

LEVEL 3

1. *The child will continue to improve his skills in asking questions about missing elements in pictures, stories, creative dramatics, and so forth.*

These improved skills should be built upon those developed in Level 2, Number 5 above. The process can now be made more systematic and deliberate. With encouragement, children at this stage can learn to ask why, how, who, what, when, is, did, will, where, and other types of questions. At times, however, they will still fall into the pattern of an overlearned or practiced question-asking skill. This is a good stage to read stories and then have the children ask questions about the characters and events that the story does not tell. I have found *Listen, Rabbit* (Fisher, 1964) to be excellent for this purpose. The story itself is quite engrossing to the children. After reading it, I use the puppet of a rabbit and play the role of the rabbit. The children begin each question with "Listen, Rabbit," and I presume the knowledge of the rabbit and try to answer their questions. Usually, the questions are quite provocative and insightful.

2. *The child will be able to identify missing elements at an increasingly complex level and to check discrepancies.*

This skill should be built upon the work done in connection with the skills in seeing missing elements in Level 2.

3. *The child will be able to order sequences of events in cartoons, photographs, and the like.*

The child's ability to state sequences at this stage is not well-developed but, with guided experiences, some definite progress can be made. Stories, events in creative dramatics, the daily schedule, and so forth provide good practice material. Complexity should not be expected at this stage. The number of events in sequence should be kept small. Some beginnings can be made in developing skills of seeing how changes in sequence change meanings.

4. *The child will begin developing skills of empathy (imagining himself in the role of another being and going beyond egocentric concerns).*

No high level of development of empathy can be expected at this stage. The child is still self-centered and egocentric but there are beginnings of empathy, and this can be increased through guided experiences. A good example of children's literary material stressing the development of empathy is the Level 3 story in *A Duck Is a Duck* (Clymer, 1963) about what to do with the turtle. The decision in the story is made on the basis of empathy for the turtle. More elaborate training in empathy can be accomplished through a literary device like the one used in Bruno Munari's *The Elephant's Wish* (1959). The elephant is tired of being a heavy, big-footed animal. When the children are asked to imagine themselves in the place of the elephant and to state what they would like to be, most of them will give egocentric responses without reference to the elephant's wish. Some will continue with these egocentric responses (their own favorite animals), while others will begin shifting to responses more relevant to the animals or birds, making the wish as the sequence unfolds showing them, through a fold-out technique, what the animal or bird was thinking. From my experience, I believe that this skill can be developed best by beginning with animals and then proceeding to chums, people, story character, and so on. These latter should probably be reserved for a later stage and not attempted at Level 3.

5. *The child will be able to recount the sequence in the creative problem-solving process.*

The story of the turtle in the park in *A Duck Is a Duck* is an excellent example of the replication of the creative problem-solving process in children's literary materials. Through guided experiences, children can be led to conceptualize the stages or sequences in the creative problem-solving process after reading such stories or engaging themselves in the sequence. Long and complex problems should be avoided at this stage.

6. *The child will accept limitations creatively rather than cynically or passively.*

Many disadvantaged children tend to give up (die early) and need to learn early the skills involved in accepting limitations creatively. Just such is implied in the theme story of *A Duck Is a Duck*.

LEVEL 4

1. *The child will develop increasingly higher level skills of producing new combinations of things and people in places.*

The helicopter story in *Helicopters and Gingerbread* (Clymer, 1969) is a good example of children's literature which shows such com-

binations. Materials should be developed to encourage children themselves to produce these new combinations.

2. *The child will become aware of more complex combinations of
sounds and will produce new combinations himself.*

3. *The child will develop increased tactual sensitivity.*

To prepare disadvantaged children to appreciate and react ade-
quately to the opening illustration, more concrete experiences in tactual
sensitivity may be needed. This may be done through the "What's in
the Bag?" technique, using feeling as the basis for identifying objects
and describing them. An example of children's literary material providing such experiences is *The Touch Me Book* (Witte, Eve and Pat,
1961).

4. *The child will be able to produce a variety of ideas about possible
functions or uses of animals, machines, etc.*

Helicopters and Gingerbread contains two good examples of multiple uses—the seal and the helicopter. The thinking to be developed here
is similar to that called for in the unusual uses and unusual questions
tasks of the *Torrance Tests of Creative Thinking.* It might be well to
provide some very fundamental, simple practice in producing ideas
about alternate uses or functions of objects, animals, and so forth that
are common to the children's experiences.

5. *The child will be able to produce alternate possible consequences
of new combinations of objects, people, places, and actions.*

This skill can be developed in relation to literary materials like
the zoo experience in *Helicopters and Gingerbread,* creative dramatics
and puppetry using the "Magic Net" approach, and the approach in
Tell a Tall Tale. Generally speaking, concentrated work on the production of possible causes should be delayed until Level 5, but some children may be ready at this stage.

6. *The child will increase his skills in empathy.*

Although it is perhaps too early to expect high levels of empathy
among children at this level, they do improve these skills with guided
sequences of experiences. Doing tasks in pairs, triads, and other team
arrangements are facilitative. Conducting telephone conversations (real
or play) may also be used. Guessing the wants or desires of an animal
in a story or in the classroom, the teacher, and so on are also facilitative.

7. *The child will increase his willingness to attempt difficult tasks.*

This skill is especially critical for disadvantaged children to learn.
A good example of children's literary materials to provide orientation

on this problem is Mary M. Green's *Is It Hard? Is It Easy?* (1960). The theme should be extended to exploration of limits within safety.

8. *The child will be able to make easy, simple predictions from limited information.*

9. *The child will develop increased skill in using his imagination in seeing and hearing things at different distances.*

10. *The child will extend his skills in asking questions about pictures and stories.*

11. *The child will produce alternative endings for stories.*

LEVEL 5

1. *The child will be able to produce and play with analogies.*

At first, pictures and models should be used in playing with the analogies. Some tentative use of analogies in stating and solving problems can be initiated, but serious work of this kind should probably be delayed for a while. For play with analogies, all four of the following types of analogies can be used: (1) *personal analogy*, personal identification with the elements of a problem, expressing it in the language most familiar to the child; (2) *direct analogy*, describing the actual comparison of parallel facts, knowledge, or technology, such as between the telephone and the human ear; (3) *symbolic analogy*, using objects and impersonal images to describe the problem; and (4) *fantasy analogy*, creating fantasies, magical solutions, and then bringing them down to earth.

2. *The child will continue developing his ability to produce alternative possible consequences.*

This may be done by having him "play with" improbable situations of the "Just Imagine" variety, such as the one shown on the next page. It may be done by placing people or story characters in different places —different countries, different climates, different resources locations, and so forth, changing one variable at a time—and having pupils think through the possible consequences. It may also be done by having pupils predict the possible outcomes of stories, or the results of changes in weather, by the substitution of one character for another, and the like. Practice can also be given in bridging the gap between a situation and a consequence.

JUST IMAGINE YOU COULD MAKE YOUR PET ANYTHING YOU WANTED!
WHAT ALL MIGHT HAPPEN?

3. *The child will begin to develop ability to produce alternative causes of behavior.*

The teacher must remember that the development of ability to produce alternative causes of behavior develops more slowly than ability to produce alternative consequences. At this level, practice can be given in producing multiple hypotheses about activities, problems, and feelings of people and animals in stories. Pupils can be encouraged to guess causes and consequences of behavior depicted in pictures and stories.

4. *The child will continue to produce alternative solutions to problems.*

This can be done with everyday problems, the problems of people and animals in stories, the problems in making original stories.

5. *The child will continue developing skills of empathy.*

Teachers must remember that the skills of empathy continue to develop rather slowly at this level. Some children at this stage, however, are emerging from their egocentrism enough to make real progress in developing empathic skills. They can be asked to empathize with characters in stories, pictures, and the like. Children can be asked to make up problems for story characters and about these characters.

6. *The child will continue developing his ability to elaborate.*

Some real progress can be made in developing ability to elaborate at this stage, but this development should not be pushed too hard just now. Children at this level can elaborate story elements, story themes, and so forth by filling in the details of a story, illustrating the story or elements of it, dramatizing story elements, and the like. They can produce variations of the events and characters in stories, and they can begin producing original dialogue for a dramatization. Elaboration can be encouraged by having children imagine a different world, creating perspective, constructing imaginary figures and background (colony on the moon, Mars, etc.; a world without the color yellow; a world without birds, etc.).

7. *The child will continue developing his ability to visualize.*

In reading stories or poems, children can be asked to visualize actions, objects, and sequences and to identify and describe incongruities. They can be encouraged to use imagery to develop the setting for a story or play.

8. *The child will begin producing unusual and novel uses.*

In encouraging children at this level to produce unusual and novel uses or functions for objects, people, animals, events, and so forth, it will take some effort to get them away from the set of "intended uses" —what it is supposed to do—to unintended but still legitimate and valuable uses.

9. *The child will begin developing ability to synthesize diverse elements.*

Beginnings can be made toward the development of ability to synthesize by having children make up titles for pictures and stories, inventing names for characters in stories, and so on.

10. *The child will continue developing his forecasting ability.*

As a story is read orally, children can be encouraged to foresee problems as they emerge in a story situation.

11. *The child will continue developing his ability to imagine feelings.*
Children at this stage can be asked to make multiple associations of feelings with color and sound.

LEVEL 6

1. *The child will continue developing his ability to infer causes and consequences of an increasing variety of behavior.*
Children at this level are likely to continue to be more skilled in inferring consequences than in inferring causes but this gap should now be becoming smaller. They should be encouraged deliberately to produce multiple hypotheses concerning the causes of the behavior of children in stories, to interpret the thoughts and actions of story characters, and the like. Ability to produce alternative consequences should now be extended to helping children become aware of problems, difficulties, conflicts, disharmonies, and the like. Children can produce alternative outcomes for stories, can make predictions from limited information, can think of the consequences of new combinations of things in their environment, and can predict the reactions of story characters in different situations. To further the development of ability to do causal thinking, children at this level enjoy producing fun-type explanations of common phenomena.

2. *The child will go beyond the obvious, superficial, and common-place and infer meanings from statements in stories, descriptions of events, and the like.*
At this level, most children are at a stage of development when they can make progress in seeing that behavior which at first seemed silly is actually quite sensible, and when they can also make progress in getting a maximum of information from a small number of clues in stories and illustrations. They can also develop an awareness of the fact that there can be a magical quality about everyday events. Most children are now able to begin going beyond the obvious in classifying familiar terms, objects, characters, and the like.

3. *The child will begin to acquire real skills in elaborating ideas—working out the details of ideas, building up an image, and filling in gaps in information.*
Skills in elaborating can be encouraged by having children elaborate on the personalities of story characters and make tentative predictions from limited information about a character in a particular situation. They can be encouraged to use story clues to interpret a character's thoughts and actions. They can elaborate story elements by

creating conversation among the characters of a story, by presenting specific information in booklet form, by drawing, dramatizing, collecting and displaying certain items, by illustrating the steps in a sequence, by writing and illustrating stories, by writing the dramatization of a story, and by making multiple associations to a word, character, or concept. This is also a good time to encourage children to elaborate story elements by describing views from different locations and different psychological or sociological viewpoints. They are also ready to use specific words in a variety of ways. Some beginnings can also be made in getting children to elaborate story detail through the use of similes.

4. *The child will begin making real progress in learning skills of empathy.*

Most children, by the time they reach this level, have emerged from their egocentrism to begin to empathize with others—to imagine themselves in another's position, to feel and to experience with another. This kind of behavior may not occur very frequently, however, unless some deliberate encouragement is given in developing the component skills. In reading, children at this level can emphathize with story characters by imagining how the characters feel about the events they are experiencing. They can imagine how they would feel and act in situations similar to those of the story characters. They can further their empathic development by imagining what questions a story character would ask about certain problems or events. They can put themselves in the roles of story characters and, by enacting them, can become aware of feelings, problems, and alternative solutions.

5. *The child will begin making real progress in developing question-asking skills.*

Unless children have had considerable deliberate and fairly intense stimulation in asking questions, few of them, prior to this level, will have developed good question-asking skills. This kind of development can be encouraged by having children produce multiple questions about story elements and pictures, analyze ambiguities and uncertainties in stories, and detect missing information.

6. *The child will be able, with guidance, to carry through the sequence of creative problem solving.*

Many children at this level will be able, with guidance, to carry through the sequence of creative problem solving with reasonable skills. Many of them will have developed some skills of becoming aware of and recognizing problems, digging into "the mess," defining a problem, brainstorming possible solutions, developing criteria for evaluating the alternative solutions, deciding upon a solution, and developing plans for implementing it. They will, of course, still need additional practice in the component skills, especially in developing criteria and using them in evaluating alternative solutions.

Children at this stage will also need help in discovering that silent times can be used for solving problems, and they will need help in applying this insight. They will also need help in developing skills for solving their own developmental problems creatively and independently, but some progress can be made. Skills at this stage may also be improved by comparing the problem-solving techniques of different story characters and by encouraging identification with children who are good problem solvers.

7. *The child will advance his skills in differentiating guesses or hypotheses from conclusions.*

Some progress will already have been made, even without deliberate effort, in differentiating guesses or hypotheses from conclusions, but structured sequences of activities designed to develop these skills should now be profitable. In the process of reading, deliberate practice should be given in checking hypotheses against new information.

8. *The child will make further progress in developing skills of synthesizing diverse elements.*

Progress in developing skills of synthesizing diverse elements may still be slow. Such skills can be encouraged at this level by having children produce alternate titles for pictures, stories, dramatizations, pantomimed presentations, and the like. Exercises in writing poetry, even simple types such as cinquains, are very useful in developing some of the component skills of synthesis.

Children at this stage can compose simple cinquains by utilizing the following pattern:

> First line — one word (the title)
> Second line — two words, describing the title
> Third line — three words, expressing an action
> Fourth line — four words, expressing a feeling
> Fifth line — another word for the title.

The development of ability to synthesize can be encouraged by having children brainstorm words for the second, third, and fourth lines and then selecting those words that best capture the essence of all the words brainstormed. The best opportunity for encouraging synthesis, however, is in finding just the right word for the fifth line—a word that pulls the entire cinquain together, summarizes it, or catches its essence.

9. *The child will continue the development of his ability to visualize objects, places, actions, people, and so forth.*

At this level, skills in visualization can be enhanced by encouraging children to imagine objects, actions, and feelings or moods created by special words. They should also be encouraged to visualize things from different vantage points and to describe objects and places from different perspectives. They should be encouraged to recognize (create) "magic pictures" formed by clouds, spotlights, constellations, signal beams, abstract paintings, and illustrations in books. Expressing ideas in pantomime and interpreting roles through pantomime can also be used to encourage the development of visualization abilities.

10. *The child will continue the development of his ability to write original stories and poems.*

Until this level, children are so limited by their handwriting, spelling, and vocabulary that they have been restricted in their ability to write imaginative and original stories, poems, plays, and the like. These abilities are still marginal, and such productions by many will still have to be dictated to an adult or to a tape recorder. Many children, however, will prefer writing their own compositions. At this level, children enjoy thinking of humorous and/or surprising endings for stories, plays, and the like. They can develop an awareness of the fact that the unexpected or incongruous often helps make a story humorous. Progress can also be made at this level by encouraging children to express a mood in poetic form, to illustrate original stories, or to produce new versions of a folktale.

11. *The child will produce alternative ideas about the relevance or application of a particular story.*

With the further development of creative problem-solving skills and play with analogies, the component skills for making applications from stories now exist and should be used.

12. *The child will build onto his existing knowledge by relating ideas in a new story to other ideas.*

It is not until later that children display a strong tendency to produce relationships between previously acquired information and ideas from new material, or between two fields such as biology and social studies. The groundwork can be laid at this stage, however, through deliberate but simple exercises in producing such relationships.

13. *The child will increase his understanding and appreciation of his curiosity.*

Children who have attained this level are frequently being subjected to pressure to reduce their curiosity behavior. Therefore, their curiosity is disparaged, making this stage an ideal one at which to develop in children an understanding and appreciation of their curiosity. Along with these attempts, of course, should go the development of increased skills in question asking and in other ways of finding out information.

Conclusion

It should be emphasized at this point that the foregoing formulation of the hierarchy of creative skills is both tentative and incomplete. As I am able to do more intense work with older children, I shall try to extend the hierarchy upward. Meanwhile, I shall try to devise ways of teaching undergraduate college students and graduate students so as to develop many of these lower level skills. I shall try increasingly to conduct experiments to validate the hypothesized hierarchy. And I shall try to develop materials in various curricular areas to implement it.

5

Building
Creative-Reading Skills

There are several controversial issues regarding the involvement of the creative-thinking processes in reading and literature. In teaching beginning reading, some teachers believe in an approach through which children make up their own stories, using them as well as those of their classmates for reading materials. These teachers emphasize imagery in connection with these and the other materials their pupils read. They also encourage their pupils to ask questions about the stories they read, especially questions that cannot be completely answered by the reading material. Many other teachers are frightened by this approach and say that it has no place in teaching children to read. *What position do you take? How would you defend your position?*

Why Read Creatively?

I believe strongly that, next to the skills involved in increased awareness and in knowing pupils, creative teaching and learning rest upon the skills of reading creatively. Thus, teachers themselves need to acquire these skills and to provide assignments to facilitate the acquisition of these skills by their pupils.

Even the acquisition of information through reading involves imagination, visualization, seeing new relationships, and the reorganization of facts. The acquisition of information, however, is not enough. Children should find most of their reading exciting and useful in solving problems and coping with the stresses of their daily lives. The ability to think is limited primarily by one's personal experiences and the uses he makes of them in problem solving, abstracting, generalizing, judging, and making decisions. The creative reader increases his personal experiences through his reading because he uses the information gained thereby very much as he would firsthand experiences. In solving problems and making decisions for action, he is about as likely to see the

relevance of a story situation or a biographical account as he is the relevance of a firsthand experience. What he reads becomes real to him, and he can use it. *This is not true of the reader who lacks the skills of reading creatively.*

"Getting the Truth" by Reading

Not only does it take a creative reader to make use of what is read, but it takes a creative reader to "get the truth" from what is read. One way of developing the reader's skills of getting the truth from what is read is by teaching him something of the nature of the intellectual process known as historiography (the research methods involved in history) and something of its scientific spirit and method. Historiography requires both critical and creative reading. Being a critical reader satisfies these requirements by making one aware of the biases and deficiencies in records and accounts by witnesses. It takes a creative reader to dig more deeply, to get behind the events, and to find out the reasons behind discrepant accounts, to synthesize them, and to reach sound conclusions about what is true.

Children catch the spirit of historiography and develop with amazing rapidity skills in the intellectual process involved. Even young children are capable of sensing discrepancies, of detecting gaps in information, of digging more deeply behind the facts, of looking at the same set of facts from different viewpoints, and of sweeping away irrelevant and false information. Vincent Rogers (1962) has created some fascinating materials in elementary social studies to develop such skills from the first grade upwards. He has described a project in which seven-year-olds collected information about the changes that had taken place during the past year on their streets, in their houses, and "downtown." Following this gathering of information, there emerged over a period of weeks considerable discussion of change and the process of change. In another project designed to develop these skills, fifth graders were confronted with several pictures of Christopher Columbus and were asked to determine which was the "real Christopher Columbus." To aid them, they were given primary sources of information such as letters written by Columbus and his contemporaries, records and accounts of Columbus' activities, and the like. The pupils usually concluded that none of the pictures fit all of the facts, since there are no existent photographs of Columbus. They were able to decide that some of the pictures fit the facts more closely than others, however.

Let us examine the nature of the process of historiography more closely and then see how it resembles what happens when a person reads creatively. The process involves at least the following:

1. An awareness of the existence and nature of problems that may be solved historically.

2. A recognition of the functions and limitations of the historical methods.
3. A readiness to collect and to submit to careful examination the available evidence needed to test the validity of any statement.
4. A willingness to give proper consideration to various pieces of information.
5. A recognition of one's own biases and efforts to eliminate their effects.
6. A determination to make only such conclusions as are justified by the evidence.

The development of skills in this process involves constant practice in causal thinking, in producing and testing hypotheses about causes and consequences. In this way, a child can begin to learn early that although cause and consequence are related by temporal succession, temporal succession does not constitute causation. He can learn to seek the historical causes of an event among the various temporal antecedents of an event rather than among its simultaneous conditions and consequences. He can learn to treat every statement of causal connection as an hypothesis to be tested for internal consistency against other pieces of information. He can learn that the solution of a given problem may require controlled experimentation and that no one method of searching for the truth is supreme.

Remembering What Is Read

Even after the validity of a piece of information has been determined and the "truth of the matter" decided, it takes a creative reader to remember it in a meaningful way. In this connection, it is interesting to note that almost all of the special courses for improving one's memory bring into play the creative-thinking abilities and processes. The methods used in these memory-improvement courses evoke visual and/or auditory imagery associated with what is to be remembered, multiple associations to whatever is to be remembered, and the formation of new relationships among the materials to be remembered.

Attitude toward What Is Read

In evaluating the importance of developing the skills of reading creatively, it should be remembered that it is not the amount of information per se that one possesses which enables him to find satisfactory solutions. The thing that is important is the way the information has been stored and one's attitude toward it. Torrance and Harmon (1961) have demonstrated this point by having college students read research articles creatively as opposed to reading them critically, and by having them read textbook materials with different reading sets.

What Happens in Creative Reading?

When researchers conduct experiments such as the ones just mentioned, it becomes necessary to describe the process of reading creatively. The researchers try to establish what they call a "creative set." The instructions given by Torrance (1965a) in the experiment involving the critical and creative reading of research reports is as follows, and the reader might try it on himself in carrying out some assignment to get a better understanding of its meaning:

> When you read, it is important that you think about the many possible uses of the information which you are reading. It is especially important that you think of the various ways in which information could be used in your personal and professional life. In reading, do not just ask, "What is the author saying?" Also ask, "How can I use what the author is saying?" Do not stop with just one use. Think of as many possible uses as you can of the important ideas presented. Jot down these possible uses for future reference. It may take some practice before you are really successful in assuming this set or attitude toward your reading, but do not be discouraged. Keep trying. By the third day, you should find it fairly easy to assume this set.

Those who assumed the *critical* set or attitude were asked to describe the *defects* in the statement of the problem of the research article and its importance, the underlying assumptions and hypotheses studied, procedures for collecting and analyzing the data, the conclusions and interpretation of the findings, and a critical appraisal of the worth of the research. The *creative* readers were asked to think of new possibilities suggested by the problem, other possible hypotheses related to the problem, improvements that could have been made in collecting and analyzing the data, other possible conclusions and interpretations of the findings, and an appraisal of the possibilities stemming from the findings. Students reading research reports creatively produced new ideas that were judged to be more creative than those of their peers who read critically. Each student read and evaluated five articles, and then developed a new idea of his own, not necessarily related to any of the articles.

One way of conceptualizing the mental processes that occur when one reads creatively is in terms of the operation of the mental abilities involved. The creative reader sensitizes himself to problems, gaps in information, missing elements, discordant elements, something incorrect or ugly. This sets in motion tensions or pressures that call for the formation of new relationships and combinations, synthesizing relatively unrelated elements into a coherent whole, redefining or transforming certain elements to discover new uses, and building onto what is known. In this search for solutions or reduction of tension, several important activities are present: the production of a large number of possibilities or hypotheses (*fluency*); the use of many different approaches or strategies (*flexibility*); the production of bold new ideas off the beaten path or the making of mental leaps (*originality*); and the development of an idea, filling out the details, making the idea attractive or embroidering it (*elaboration*).

Many suggestions have been made as to how the reader produces these ideas. Almost all agree that in order to produce ideas, the creative reader must be open to his experiences. He must keep himself "loose." He must reflect upon what he reads, discovering new relationships among the ideas presented and seeing them in the light of his own experiences. He must react to new ideas, playing with the possibility that a new idea might be correct, and then try to visualize or predict what its consequences might be. In this way, the new idea becomes a center of vivid, concrete images and feeling reactions. The creative reader assumes an inquiring attitude about what he reads and seeks to make rational evaluations.

The creative reader also tends to identify with the author or with a character in the story, play, or novel that he is reading. Through the imaginative processes of identification and empathy, the creative reader can predict what is going to happen next and what might have happened instead. This leaves the creative reader with a desire, perhaps a need, to discuss the material in his own unique terms or to transform the experience himself into a poem, a song, a dance form, a picture, or a drama.

How Do Creative Readers Develop?

Creative readers develop through procedures that heighten expectations and anticipation and that give practice in doing something with what is read, either at the time it is being read or afterwards.

The creative process itself embodies the tension of anticipation or expectation. It has variously been described as the warming-up process; the ability to rise to the occasion; or attraction to the unknown, the strange, and the puzzling. The arousal of anticipation involves reactions to the reading material before, during, and after the actual reading. The major problem is to use this arousal to see the fundamental relationships among the facts, ideas, and events that constitute the reading materials, and the experiences and problems of the reader.

Doing something with what is read may be conceptualized at four levels: reproducing literary material imaginatively by oral reading, elaborating what is read, rearranging and transforming what is read, and going beyond what is read.

Even if one's job is only to reproduce what is read, the creative-thinking abilities can be called into play. What is read can be reproduced mechanically, or it can be reproduced with imagination—feeling oneself into the actions, emotions, thinking, images, sounds, and odors expressed. John Ciardi's (1962) *I Met a Man* expresses this idea quite well. This recording grew out of Ciardi's own attempts to teach his children to read with imagination. One child was reading slowly and laboriously. The other was reading with extreme rapidity. Both were reading mechanically. In this recording, Ciardi encourages children to read as though the thing is happening.

The second level beyond reproducing what is read is that of elaborating on what is read—filling in the gaps imaginatively on the basis of the information given, predicting from the known facts. Some reading specialists like Durrell and Chambers (1958) believe that exercises and instructional materials that encourage elaborative thinking are especially valuable. They believe that elaborative thinking in connection with reading produces higher permanent retention and greater availability of knowledge to new situations. They include elaborative thinking in its many forms, such as relating the content of reading to previous knowledge, illustrations and applications, opportunities for use or practice, relationships to other fields, and various associations that integrate reading into knowledge or action. They think that elaborative thinking is better done in discussion groups of various sizes than in either individual or whole-class activities, that specific planning or applications are better than remote or academic tasks.

The third level of doing something with what is read is that of transforming and rearranging what is read to form new combinations. A good illustration of this level is the work of William Shakespeare. He rarely invented new plots or characters. He borrowed them from history, mythology, and legends, but he transformed them so creatively and aesthetically, with such depth of understanding and truth, that his plays are still recognized as great creative achievements. Again, this ability to transform and rearrange is itself a valuable tool in coping with the demands of life, as well as in the achievement of outstanding productions.

On the fourth level of going beyond what is read, the reader uses what he reads as a stepping-stone to new ideas, as a source of inspiration, as a mainspring of new ideas, and as an impetus to a further search for the truth through additional reading, questioning, or experimentation. The mental process is much like what creative problem solvers call "hitchhiking." A person reads something in a field quite different from the body of knowledge in which a problem is set. This kind of reading may send the reader completely out of the field in which he is reading to solutions for problems that have been of long concern to him.

What Can Teachers Do to Facilitate Creative Reading?

In planning exercises to facilitate creative reading, it is useful to think in terms of what can be done before, during, and after the reading to heighten anticipation and expectation, and to encourage the reader to do something with what he reads. On the basis of an analysis of the kinds of practice that result in creative growth and that facilitate creative functioning, I have prepared an inventory of the kinds of things that teachers can do before, during, and after a lesson to facilitate the creative functioning and development of pupils.

This inventory is presented below and will be elaborated upon in the next three chapters of this book. No teacher will ever want to use all the ideas suggested by this inventory with a single lesson, and there is some overlapping among the categories. The large number of ideas and the overlapping have been retained because the inventory is intended as a source for generating ideas about activities before, during, and after almost any kind of lesson, not just a reading lesson. In fact, most of the ideas can be used in art, music, social studies, science, and other curricular elements.

Characteristics of Learning Experiences to Facilitate Creative Behavior

A. *Activities before Lesson (Reading)*
1. Confrontation with ambiguities and uncertainties precipitated.
2. Anticipation and expectation heightened.
3. Awareness of problem to be solved, difficulty to be faced, gap in information to be filled, etc. heightened.
4. Building onto existing information or skills facilitated.
5. Concern about a problem heightened.
6. Curiosity and wanting to know stimulated.
7. Familiar made strange or strange made familiar by analogy.
8. Freedom from inhibiting sets facilitated.
9. Looking at same material from several different psychological or sociological viewpoints promoted.
10. Provocative questions requiring learner to examine information in a different way and in greater depth asked.
11. Predictions from limited information required.
12. Purposefulness of activity made clear.
13. Assignment structured only enough to give clues and direction.
14. Taking the next step beyond what is known encouraged.
15. Warm-up provided in some way (easy to difficult, familiar to unfamiliar, bodily involvement, etc.).

B. *Activities during Lesson (Reading)*
1. Awareness of problems and difficulties heightened during progress of lesson.
2. Creative and constructive rather than cynical acceptance of limitations in information, skills, etc. facilitated.
3. Creative personality characteristics or predispositions (willingness to attempt the difficult, freedom to conform or nonconform, etc.) encouraged.
4. Creative problem-solving process replicated in stories, accounts of history and invention, etc.
5. Creative processes described, illustrated, and illuminated in stories, historical accounts, etc.
6. Exploration made deliberate and systematic.
7. Incompleteness of information presented.
8. Juxtaposition of apparently irrelevant elements precipitated.
9. Mysteries explored and examined.
10. Open-endedness preserved.
11. Outcomes not completely predictable.
12. Predictions from limited information required.
13. Reading with imagination (to make it sound like the thing happening) encouraged.
14. Search for truth facilitated by honesty and realism of materials.
15. Skills for finding out identified and encouraged.
16. Surprises heightened and deliberately used.
17. Visualization encouraged.

C. *Activities after Lesson (Reading)*
1. Ambiguities played with.
2. Awareness of problem, difficulty, gap in information, etc. facilitated.
3. Awareness and acknowledgment by teachers of pupil potentialities based on response.
4. Concern about problem heightened.
5. Constructive response called for (other ways, better ways, etc.).
6. Continuity with previously learned skills, information, etc. facilitated.
7. Constructive rather than cynical acceptance of limitations encouraged.
8. Digging more deeply required, going beyond the obvious.
9. Divergent thinking made legitimate.
10. Elaborating upon what is read encouraged.
11. Elegant solutions (simplest solutions taking into account largest number of variables) encouraged.

12. Empathic metaphor to give new feeling or understanding of object, person, or state facilitated.
13. Experimentation required.
14. Familiar made strange or strange made familiar by analogy.
15. Fantasies examined to find solutions to realistic problems.
16. Future projection encouraged.
17. Going beyond text materials encouraged.
18. Improbabilities entertained.
19. Irrelevance (apparently) accepted and used.
20. Judgment deferred until pool of ideas has been produced.
21. Knowledge from one field brought to bear on another.
22. Looking at same material from several different viewpoints encouraged.
23. Manipulation of ideas, objects, information encouraged.
24. Multiple hypotheses encouraged.
25. One thing permitted to lead to another.
26. Paradoxes confronted and examined.
27. Play in pushing a fundamental law to its limit encouraged.
28. Possible causes and consequences called for.
29. Provocative questions used.
30. Potentialities discovered and tested.
31. Reorganization of information required.
32. Returning to previously acquired skill, information, etc. to see new relationships encouraged.
33. Self-initiated learning encouraged.
34. Skills for finding out practiced.
35. Synthesis of different and apparently irrelevant elements facilitated.
36. Systematic testing of hypotheses encouraged.
37. Taking next step beyond what is known facilitated.
38. Testing and revision of predictions provided.
39. Transformation and rearrangement of materials encouraged.

6

Heightening Anticipation

Fundamental to any creative act is the warm-up process. The warm-up process is highly dependent upon the kind and degree of the novelty to be met. Consequently, whatever is done to heighten anticipation before reading a story or poem, or before any classroom activity, should facilitate the warm-up process and thus encourage creative behavior in dealing with the reading material, experiment, discussion, or other classroom activity.

Moreno (1946), through his work with psychodrama, sociodrama, and role playing, has provided some very provocative ideas about the warm-up process in relation to creativity and spontaneity. In psychodrama and sociodrama, Moreno uses the novelty of the situation as one of the features of warm-up. The plots, the persons, the objects in the situation, its time and space, and so forth are all novel to the actor entering the psychodramatic situation. Moreno has dealt with two kinds of self-starters, physical starters and mental starters. According to him, the infant makes use only of physical starters, and thus physical starters continue to be the "rescue-starters" in all warming-up processes throughout the life span. This perhaps is the reason I have found that physical warm-up activities are especially helpful in encouraging creativity among preschool children and disadvantaged children. Moreno points out that adults resort to physical starters in emergencies and when taken by surprise.

Moreno explains (1946, pp. 54-55) that, as a person develops, he acquires a variety of mental, social, and psychochemical starters. These may independently initiate a person's warming-up, or they may interact with physical starters. Even the infant is capable of a considerable degree of self-starting, but some infants need more help than others. In psychodrama, Moreno uses "auxiliary egos" (other actors playing supporting roles) to help the actor warm up and to achieve higher levels of creative and constructive behavior. The co-action between the actor

Photograph by Follow Through, Atlanta Public Schools

and the auxiliary ego or egos facilitates the learning of the actor. The ideas suggested in this chapter are designed to achieve much the same purpose for the classroom learner as the auxiliary egos in Moreno's psychodrama. The ideas suggested here include both physical and mental starters, but primarily mental ones. If a teacher is working with very young, disadvantaged, emotionally disturbed, or mentally retarded children or youth, greater reliance should probably be placed on physical starters than on mental ones.

In this chapter, I have given an illustration of an activity that might be used before reading a story entitled "You Can Depend on Bill" from a reading book (Clymer and Neff, 1969) used at about the third grade level. Similar activities can be invented for use in any subject, with almost any story or poem, or any learning activity. For economy, however, it seemed desirable to base all of the illustrations on a single story.

The story, "You Can Depend on Bill," is set on one city block. Mr. Lester, the shoe repairman, asks Bill, the errand boy at Miss Ada's dress shop, to help his daughter, Bonny, to cross the street at Miss Ada's corner on the way to school. Bonny likes to "dillydally," looking at the dresses in Miss Ada's shop window. Although the dresses are expensive and only for adult women, Bonny longs for one. When Bill tells Miss Ada about Bonny's problem, Miss Ada designs and makes a dress to fit Bonny and sells it to her for the dimes and pennies she has saved by sweeping the floor of her father's shop. The story illustrates the interdependence among Bonny, Bill, Miss Ada, and Mr. Lester.

1. CONFRONTATION WITH AMBIGUITIES AND UNCERTAINTIES

As in most elementary school reading books, the story title and the opening illustration provide ready-made opportunities for confronting ambiguities and uncertainties before reading. Especially for ghetto children and other disadvantaged youngsters, the illustrations in reading books are filled with ambiguities and uncertainties. Children who have not been brought up in homes where there are books containing pictures have great difficulty in interpreting pictures. Confronting these ambiguities and uncertainties can be used both to develop skills in reading a picture and to motivate creative reading.

Although the ambiguity and uncertainty of the first illustration is rather low, a teacher might simply ask children to interpret the picture —tell what is happening, who the people are, what they are like, and so on. A similar approach would be to ask the children what they can tell "for sure" just from the picture and what uncertain inferences they can draw. The uncertainties can be used to motivate reading.

A second approach would be to encourage pupils to ask as many questions as they can about the picture—things that they cannot find out from just looking at the picture.

A third approach would be to ask children directly some of the questions that children themselves ask about the picture. In some cases, the question can be answered by reading the selection the picture illustrates or by additional reading in encyclopedias and other sources. Still others cannot be answered. It is especially valuable to teach children to look for puzzling things in a picture and to ask questions about them.

The first illustration may present third grade children with difficulties in perspective. The tall building behind Miss Ada's, the TV antennae and clothes lines, and the lavender awning on Miss Ada's shop that extends in front of the stoplight may be especially puzzling. Does the awning really extend out over the sidewalk beyond the stoplight pole? Is the stoplight pole transparent? Or, has the artist been inaccurate in his representation of these relationships?

2. Anticipation and Expectation Heightened

In a sense, all of the "Activities before Reading" represent efforts to heighten anticipation and expectation, but most of them have additional objectives. Since we are trying to maximize the generation of ideas, it seems desirable to retain "Anticipation and Expectation Heightened" as a separate category in spite of the redundancy it introduces.

On the basis of the title, "You Can Depend on Bill," the teacher could heighten anticipation by such questions as: What kind of story do you expect this to be? Who do you think depends on Bill? Why do they depend on him? How old do you suppose Bill is? Is he old enough to be depended upon? In what kind of place do you think Bill lives? Are other boys there dependable?

3. Awareness of a Problem to Be Solved, a Difficulty to Be Faced

The title of a selection and the illustrations can all be used to create an awareness of gaps in information, a problem to be solved, or a difficulty to be faced, but they do not themselves pose problems or difficulties. Therefore, this type of learning experience can be constructed most readily by going to one of the central problems or difficulties of the story. For example, the problem could be set something like the following: "In this story, a little girl named Bonny, a woman named Miss Ada, and a man named Mr. Lester all depended on Bill. Bill was probably only about eight or nine years old and did not have much money. How could these people depend upon anyone like that?"

The problem can also be stated more generally in terms of all the things that the reader (a third grade child) can be depended upon to do and to be. To increase involvement, the teacher may ask, "Who depends upon you? What can they depend upon you to do?" Another approach would be to ask, "Do you know a boy that you can depend

upon? Why can you depend upon him?" Such questions can set the stage
for making this lesson one in social responsibility. William Glasser in
Schools without Failure (1969) gives a place of prime importance to the
teaching of social responsibility in working with disadvantaged children.
He believes that this is one of their greatest needs.

4. Building onto the Individual's or Group's Existing Knowledge

The best learning experiences that build onto the children's existing
knowledge will grow out of the teacher's interaction with children and
his knowledge of what they know and want to know. There are several activities that can be built upon previous selections in *How It Is
Nowadays*. All of the stories could be reviewed for examples of interdependence. The children's personal "knowing" can also be used. The
teacher could ask the children to give examples from their own experiences (both negative and positive) of depending upon others or of being
depended upon. It might be productive to ask, "Did anyone ever depend upon you to do something that you could not do?" As examples
are given, the teacher might question further, "Even though you, yourself, could not do what was expected of you, was there anything you
could have done?" Then the entire class might brainstorm for things
that the child could have done.

5. Concern about a Problem Heightened

"You Can Depend on Bill" is a good example of a story that helps
children cope with the problems of development. With this story, the
problems sketched under 4 above could be elaborated in such a way
as to heighten concern about being dependable and about depending
upon others. Again, the most effective activities are likely to grow out
of the problems of the children. In some ghetto schools, young children
are subjected to the pressures of protection rackets operated by older
children. If this is true in a given school, discussions about depending
upon other boys and girls might bring this problem to the teacher's
attention.

6. Curiosity and Wanting to Know Stimulated

A number of the activities already suggested might be pursued in
such a way as to arouse curiosity and wanting to know. It can be done
with the new words encountered in the story—words like "dillydally"
and "pumps." It can also be done by pointing out puzzling features in
the illustrations. In the first illustrations, why do you suppose the two
children are the only people outside on this busy city block?

Curiosity and wanting to know can also be aroused in relation to
one of the sub-problems of the story. "In this story, Bonny dillydallied

in front of a shop that sold only expensive dresses for grown-up ladies. Bonny was only about eight years old and had only the dimes and pennies her father gave her for sweeping his shoe repair shop. Why did she continue to dillydally?" The following questions might be asked about the illustration showing Bonny buying the dress from Miss Ada: "How did this dress for a little girl get in a store that sells only grown-up ladies' dresses?" "Bonny had enough dimes and pennies to buy the dress, but you can't see any money in the jar. How can you explain this?"

7. FAMILIAR MADE STRANGE OR STRANGE MADE FAMILIAR

What is familiar to the children in one school may be unfamiliar in another. Therefore, good exercises on making the familiar strange and the strange familiar have to grow out of the subcultures and locale of the children being taught. Most urban children, however, are likely to be familiar with city blocks like the one pictured and described in "You Can Depend on Bill." To make the story real, the children might be asked to think of a block in their neighborhood most like the one in this story. If shoe repair shops like Lester's and clothing stores like Miss Ada's are strange to the children reading the story, arrangements might be made for them to visit similar shops and find out how shoes are repaired, how dresses are designed and made, and so on. To further this process, the girls might be encouraged to design and make dresses for a doll. Or, both boys and girls might be encouraged to participate in a project to repair outgrown dolls or other toys to give to younger children. The girls could design and make new clothes for the dolls, and perhaps the boys could repaint or retouch the paint on some of the dolls and repair their shoes.

8. FREE FROM INHIBITING SETS

One inhibiting set in some classes reading "You Can Depend on Bill" might stem from the racial mix made apparent by the illustrations. It is rather clear that Bonny and Mr. Lester are black and that Miss Ada is white. Bill might be of Mexican, American Indian, Puerto Rican, or other origin. Therefore, any exercise to help children recognize the interdependence of races might free them from this inhibiting set. Some children might also have the inhibiting set that work like Bill's running errands for Miss Ada and Bonny's sweeping the floor of the shoe repair shop are unpleasant and degrading. An exercise about the pleasure and importance of doing small jobs well might free children from this inhibiting set. Such problems as these could be discussed freely and openly before reading the story, if such inhibiting sets exist in a class.

9. LOOKING AT THE SAME MATERIAL FROM DIFFERENT VIEWPOINTS

Before reading the story, the teacher might ask each pupil to take some role, to imagine himself as being Bonny, Bill, Mr. Lester, Miss Ada, a customer of Miss Ada, a customer of Mr. Lester, the owner of John's Discount Store, or the like. As they read the story, they could then be encouraged to imagine how they (as Bonny or Bill, etc.) would react to what happens. What would interest them? What lesson would they get from the story? What would it mean to them? How would they interpret each action of the others?

10. PROVOCATIVE QUESTIONS

Some of the questions already suggested might become provocative since they are designed to make the reader or the listener think about the story or the problem of the story in a different way. Both before and during the reading of the story, a series of provocative questions could be asked to get the reader to imagine what the different characters are feeling and thinking but not expressing as the action unfolds. How did Bonny feel when Bill tried to urge her along and keep her from dillydallying? How did Miss Ada feel when she noticed Bonny dillydallying in front of her store? How did Mr. Lester feel about Bonny's using her dimes and pennies to buy the new dress?

A kind of provocative question that might help third graders to get at the heart of the problem would be: "Can a person who does not depend upon others be dependable? Why?"

11. PREDICTION FROM LIMITED INFORMATION REQUIRED

Before the reading of the story, an exercise requiring predictions from limited information might be structured something like the following: "In this story, a little girl wants a dress like the ones in Miss Ada's shop, but the dresses there are only for grown-up ladies and are very expensive. Will this little girl get the dress she wants?" Or, "The little girl said, 'You can depend on Bill.' What do you suppose Bill did that caused her to say this?"

12. PURPOSEFULNESS OF ACTIVITY MADE CLEAR

Studies of the learning difficulties of disadvantaged children, and of school dropouts, and studies of reading problems have repeatedly shown the roots to lie in feelings of purposelessness. Thus it would seem that more needs to be done in work with disadvantaged children than with advantaged children to give purpose to creative activities in reading. With some elaboration, many of the activities already proposed for use with "You Can Depend on Bill" could be used to give purpose to the reading of the story and to increase the chances that creative reading will occur. One activity to emphasize purposeful reading might be structured something like the following: "We all want to be dependable and to make other people feel that they can depend upon us. There are times when we just can't do the things we want to do to help other people. We don't have the money. We are not strong enough or big enough. Or, we don't know enough. Let us find out from this story what Bill did when he couldn't get Bonny what she wanted very badly."

13. STRUCTURED ONLY ENOUGH TO GIVE CLUES AND DIRECTIONS

To facilitate creative thinking, questions must be open-ended. Instructions must provide only enough structure to give clues and directions to the reader's behavior. Herein lies the motivating power of creative activities. Some children require a great deal more structure than others, and so the teacher must always be prepared to change the degree of structure and adapt it to meet the needs of particular pupils. A highly structured activity with "You Can Depend on Bill" would be to make a list of all the things Bill did that showed "you can depend on him." A less structured exercise would be to read the story to find out how people in a big city depend on one another, or to find out how somebody can be more dependable by depending on somebody else.

14. TAKING THE NEXT STEP BEYOND WHAT IS KNOWN

This principle is perhaps more easily applied to factual material than to stories, but it can also be applied to the development of concepts. With "You Can Depend on Bill," a teacher might want to expand his pupils' concept of dependability. By using a variety of positive and negative examples of dependable behavior, the teacher could find out how mature their concepts of dependability are. Then, the reading and discussion of Bill's behavior could be used to expand their concepts, whatever they might be, to a more mature level. In doing this, the teacher would be helping them to stretch their minds and fill gaps in their understanding of dependable behavior.

15. WARM-UP PROVIDED IN SOME WAY

Some of the exercises already proposed might provide warm-ups of the easy-to-difficult and familiar-to-unfamiliar type. Invitations to predict and imagine also aid in the warm-up process. Many disadvantaged children, however, tend to be physical learners and require some kind of physical or bodily warm-up. For example, the teacher might have pupils role play several different situations in which one child is expected to do something for someone else, something that he is incapable of doing. Then their successes and failures can be used as motivation for reading to find out how Bill handled problems like these. Frequently, music or creative movement may be used to facilitate physical warm-up for a creative activity. In the present case, "The Impossible Dream" from *Man of La Mancha* (Leigh and Dorion, 1966) might be used for such a warm-up. (After the story has been read, the class could discuss the relationships they see between the story and "The Impossible Dream" of Don Quixote, the Man of La Mancha.) A tape recording of the different noises heard on the block where Bill works—the shoe repair shop, the fish market, the hardware store, the food store, and so on—could also be used as a warm-up experience for this story.

Some readers will feel that there is too much redundancy in the foregoing categories and in those that follow. It must be remembered, however, that the purpose of these categories, principles, or strategies is to trigger ideas that will facilitate the generation of activities to encourage creative functioning. Thus, I have discouraged the collapsing or combination of categories and attempts to develop a simpler structure from the overall conceptualization. If the purpose was to classify activities for research analysis, the problem would be different.

It is suggested that the reader select some lesson at the grade level that interests him and try to create exercises to illustrate each of the above fifteen ways of heightening anticipation before a lesson or at its beginning.

7

Encountering the Unexpected and Deepening Expectations

For creative behavior, it is not enough to heighten anticipation. Warm-up is necessary, but it is not enough! The surprise of the unanticipated must be encountered. Otherwise, previously learned responses are adequate, and creative responses are not required. As a lesson unfolds or as a literary selection is read, the heightened anticipation must find fulfillment. The warm-up must be sustained. There must be the unexpected to keep the process going. Heightened anticipation must turn into deepened expectations. The activities or strategies suggested in this chapter are designed to accomplish these purposes during the process of a lesson or the reading of a literary selection. Again, the illustrations are designed for use with the story, "You Can Depend on Bill" (Clymer and Neff, 1969).

Many of the creative activities that occur during reading are either triggered by the activities that take place before reading or by the qualities of the reading material. The latter are provided for through the careful selection of material for inclusion in the readers. In oral reading, the teacher can intervene to generate creative activities as the reading progresses. This can also be done through the addition of relevant pictures, drawings, sounds, and the like interspersed in the reading. Although there is little precedent for it, it is also possible to pose new questions or problems in reading material at appropriate points. The following illustrative examples are built around "You Can Depend on Bill."

1. Awareness of Problems and Difficulties Heightened

Instead of trying to heighten awareness of problems and difficulties before the reading is begun, there are times when it is better to introduce such exercises during the process of oral reading. In "You Can Depend on Bill," the problems of Bonny's great desire for a dress from Miss Ada's shop and of Bill's apparent helplessness could be introduced. The children might even brainstorm ideas for helping Bonny, develop criteria for evaluating these ideas, and finally choose one to be developed.

2. CREATIVE AND CONSTRUCTIVE RATHER THAN CYNICAL ACCEPTANCE OF LIMITATIONS

A central idea in "You Can Depend on Bill" is that the solution of problems, the achievement of dreams, requires constructive and creative acceptance of limitations rather than cynical acceptance of them. Bonny could have accepted Bill's caution that "those ladies' dresses are too big for you," but she kept sweeping the floor of the shoe repair shop and saving her pennies and dimes. When the time came, she was prepared to buy the dress of her dreams.

Research repeatedly brings out the fact that disadvantaged children are not accustomed to viewing adults as sources of help or information. This research also emphasizes their great difficulty in delaying gratification (saving pennies and dimes in order to achieve some dream at a later time). Developing habits of creative and constructive acceptance of limitations might help reduce these deficits among disadvantaged children.

3. CREATIVE PERSONALITY CHARACTERISTICS OR PREDISPOSITIONS ENCOURAGED

By emphasizing or identifying with a creative character in a story, children can experience creative characteristics and predispositions. While Bill and Bonny are not outstanding models of creative behavior, they do manifest a number of characteristics common to creative personalities, and these might be highlighted. Bill kept a degree of openness about Bonny's desire for a dress from Miss Ada's shop. He defined the problem very honestly to Miss Ada: "She's too small for your dresses and besides they cost too much." This gave Miss Ada an idea for solving the problem, and Bill helped her implement it. Bonny displayed important creative characteristics such as not being easily discouraged, determination, unwillingness to give up a difficult plan (one considered impossible by others), and preparing for possibilities. Third grade children might see still others as they read the story.

4. CREATIVE PROBLEM-SOLVING PROCESS REPLICATED IN STORIES

At first I thought it might be difficult to find suitable stories for children, stories that make explicit the creative problem-solving process, but this has not proved to be the case. The process of creative problem solving is not as obvious in "You Can Depend on Bill" as it is in many other stories. This is perhaps because the problem-solving process here is a group process involving not only Bill, but Mr. Lester, Miss Ada, and Bonny. Each deals with the problem in his own way and contributes his part to understanding the difficulty, getting facts, defining the problem, finding a solution, and implementing it. It is just as important that the group problem-solving process be made explicit as it is to make the individual problem-solving process explicit.

Even if a story does not replicate the creative problem-solving process, this process can be built onto most stories. This can be done by stopping the reading at appropriate places to get children to:

provide needed information,
state the real problem or difficulty,
produce alternative solutions,
develop criteria for judging them,
evaluate them through the use of these criteria,
select a solution,
and implement it.

5. CREATIVE PROCESS DESCRIBED AND ILLUMINATED BY THE STORY

This need not be required of all stories, but it would be helpful to provide a few good models through stories in which the characters use deliberate methods of creative problem solving. This is perhaps easier to do in readers at the more advanced level. It is not impossible at the lower levels, as illustrated by "What Is It?" in *A Duck Is a Duck* (Clymer, 1969).

6. EXPLORATION MADE DELIBERATE AND SYSTEMATIC

In most stories, solutions to problems seem to spring full-blown from the minds of the characters or else to occur by accident. Usually, little attention is given to the processes by which the solutions come forth. This leads to an awe of the "masterpieces" or clever solutions, and it discourages the deliberate and systematic exploration necessary for creative behavior. When exploration is not made explicit in a story, children can be encouraged to engage in this exploration by filling in imaginatively as they read. This requires deliberate reading and pauses for reflective thinking rather than speed reading. In the problem of "You Can Depend on Bill," pauses could be made to try to recapture the silent, unverbalized thinking of Bonny, Bill, Miss Ada, and Mr. Lester in regard to Bonny's desire for a dress from Miss Ada's shop.

7. INCOMPLETENESS OF KNOWLEDGE PRESENTED

This category is appropriate primarily when applied to factual material. Almost any story, however, contains gaps in information, and these can be used effectively to stimulate further reading and investigation. Gaps in knowledge about designing fashions, buying for a clothing shop, the interaction among store owners and employees, and the like can be generated from "You Can Depend on Bill." Techniques for finding out such things can also be identified and cultivated.

8. Juxtaposition of Apparently Irrelevant Elements

The following are a few examles of juxtaposition of apparently irrelevant elements in "You Can Depend on Bill":

a. Bonny knew that Miss Ada sold only grown-up ladies dresses and that none of the dresses in the shop would fit her. Why did Bonny keep dillydallying in front of Miss Ada's shop and saying that some day she was going to buy one of the dresses?
b. Most dress shops sell dresses for children as well as for grown-ups. Why did Miss Ada sell only grown-up dresses?
c. Expensive dress shops are usually not located near fish markets, shoe repair shops, and outdoor fruit stands. Why do you suppose Miss Ada's shop was located in such a place?

9. Mysteries Explored and Examined

An element of mystery can be built into almost any story. "You Can Depend on Bill" is not a mystery story, but it is possible to infuse into it several elements of mystery. For example, there is an element of mystery about the characters and the setting of the story. Why do Bonny and her father live behind their shoe repair shop? If the block where the story takes place is full of too many people, why do the street and the windows look so empty? Why are there so many television antennae over the hardware store? What kind of family does Bill have? How did Bill learn to be dependable? Why did Miss Ada make such a fine dress for Bonny and sell it to her so cheaply?

10. Open-Endedness Preserved

There are many open ends in "You Can Depend on Bill." We do not know why Bonny wanted a dress from Miss Ada's shop. There must have been some shops with girls' dresses nearby. We do not know why Bill ran errands for Miss Ada. We do not know what Mr. Lester thought about Bonny's buying the dress, or even what he thought about Bill's running back to the shoe repair shop to get Bonny's money jar. We do not know how Bill and Bonny liked school. We do not know how Bonny felt about sweeping the floor of the shoe repair shop, nor whether or not she will continue to sweep it now that she has the beloved dress. All of these and other open ends give free rein to the imagination of the reader and help him to think in terms of possibilities, looking more deeply into experience.

11. Outcomes Not Completely Predictable

It would be interesting to a class to find out just what proportion of them could predict accurately whether or not Bonny would get the dress she wanted so badly from Miss Ada's shop and/or how she would get it. This might lead to a discussion of the reasons that their predictions were not 100 percent accurate. For example, they may predict in terms of their own experiences, thinking that everyone's lives are like their own.

12. Predictions from Limited Information

Several possible exercises involving predictions from limited information have already been suggested. Exercises of this type can be introduced during the process of reading just as has been suggested for before reading. At various points, the teacher can ask, "What do you think will happen now?" or "What do you think Bill will do now?" Usually, the predictions called for in the process of reading should be ones that can be checked upon through reading the remainder of the selection. And yet respect needs to be shown for plausible correct answers that reflect thinking, and for answers which show excellent insights that merit recognition and acknowledgment.

13. Reading with Imagination

Both silent and oral reading can be done with imagination and can bring into play visual imagery, sounds, smells, and other sensations. Imagine how Miss Ada's dress shop smelled and how the colorful dresses looked in her window. Imagine how Mr. Lester's shoe repair shop smelled and what sounds there were when Mr. Lester was working. Imagine how the hardware store, the fish store, and the food store smelled. Can you visualize the dimes and pennies in Bonny's glass jar? Can you imagine Bill's wink when he looked at Mr. Lester and asked, "Can Bonny deliver them? I can't wait."

Some stories are better than others for reading orally "as though the thing is happening." "You Can Depend on Bill" is perhaps only moderate in this respect. It can be enlivened, however, by such a reading because a number of lively things do happen.

14. Search for the Truth Facilitated by Honesty and Realism

The story presents an interesting and honest side of ghetto life. The story mentions the fact that some of the people on the block do not know any of the other people on the block. Bill, Bonny, Mr. Lester, and Miss Ada, however, know one another and depend upon one another. Certainly other aspects of ghetto life need to be portrayed.

Many children, however, can identify with Bill and Bonny and will know people like Miss Ada and Mr. Lester and streets like the one in the story. Even fantasies represent a kind of search for the truth, a search for explanations of human behavior and honest solutions to common human problems.

15. Skills for Finding Out Identified and Encouraged

Stories themselves can be used to show how a person can read to find out things. Miss Ada and Bill both used questions to find out some of the things they wanted to know. Disadvantaged children are severely handicapped in their ability to ask questions of adults. They are not accustomed to using adults as sources of information and have not practiced the skills of finding out by asking questions. The story of "You Can Depend on Bill" may be used to stimulate the desire to find out about shoe repairing and shoemaking, dressmaking, and selling dresses. The children might discuss ways of finding out these things and then try out some of the resulting ideas for finding out.

16. Surprises Heightened and Deliberately Used

Being alerted for surprises can make reading interesting. This may also make children become more aware of the surprise element in good stories and of ways to create surprise in writing. Children can be asked to look for and discuss the greatest surprise in the story or to make a list of things that surprised them. At different points in a story, children can be encouraged to think of ways to make that part of the story more surprising. Which is more surprising, the idea that a dependable person has to depend upon others, or that a fancy dressmaker would take time to design and make a dress for a small girl for a few pennies and dimes.

17. Visualization Encouraged

One of the great values of stories of the ghetto locale is that they are capable of eliciting a large variety of rich imagery. When stories contain rich and meaningful analogies, emphasis should be given to them. The illustrations for "You Can Depend on Bill" help the reader visualize the action. There are many gaps that the reader might visualize, however. Some stories can be enhanced by having children draw, construct models, or re-enact episodes in the stories.

8

Going Beyond Textbooks

For creativity to occur, there must be opportunities for one thing to lead to another. Therefore, it is inevitable that any genuine encouragement of creativity in the classroom must take children and young people beyond textbooks and beyond the classroom. Ideas stimulated in a reading lesson or in any other part of the curriculum might motivate a pupil to consult other people, to delve into other kinds of literature, to get out into the community, to conduct an original experiment, to write an essay or a poem, to paint an original picture, or to engage in almost any other kind of investigative or creative behavior.

The activities and strategies suggested in this chapter are designed to help teachers accomplish the goal of taking pupils beyond the textbook and, in some instances, beyond the classroom and beyond the curriculum. In general, the suggestions in this chapter are fairly conventional and will be tolerated in most schools. A number of more radical proposals have been suggested recently for taking learning beyond the classroom (Hart, 1969), and beyond the curriculum (Drews, 1968a). These more radical proposals would create a variety of new roles within the school and/or would give teachers new roles. The proposal of Elizabeth Drews (1968a) to take children and young people beyond the curriculum calls for a new kind of teacher who might be called a "teacher-counselor-consultant." This person would be an encourager or facilitator who would have an understanding of curriculum content and the nature of classroom process and interaction, and who would have insight into the growth potential of individual pupils. His function would be to work with pupils as they move toward discovery of self and toward the building of a coherent world view. The program of the school would emphasize individualization; independent study (inquiry, discovery, and self-evaluation); group discussion; encouragement of the use of more of a pupil's potential (non-symbolic learning); development of social conscience; aesthetic appreciation and ex-

pression; development of a philosophy of life; self-affirmation and commitment; use of resources rather than curriculum; an expanded realm of knowledge; direct experience; and theories and structures of knowledge. Drews believes that most high schools and colleges inhibit curiosity and motivation for continued learning.

While the proposal of Drews would require drastic reorganization of education as it now exists, I am offering in this chapter some suggested strategies for activities after a lesson. I believe that these strategies can be instrumental in accomplishing some of the same goals within the framework of the traditional classroom as it now exists. This does not mean that these goals might not be achieved more easily and speedily in a more flexible school organization. I believe, nevertheless, that an imaginative and "fully alive" teacher even now can do much to take children and young people successfully beyond textbooks, the classroom, and the curriculum.

1. AMBIGUITIES PLAYED WITH

After a story has been read, it is a good time for a group of readers to play with some of the apparent ambiguities and uncertainties with which they were confronted before reading. In addition to those already mentioned in Chapter 7, the following are some ambiguities in "You Can Depend on Bill" that might be played with:

  a. Did Miss Ada live and work in the back rooms of her shop as Bonny and Mr. Lester did?
  b. Did Bill live at Miss Ada's or just work there in the afternoons?
  c. Did Bill know any of the other people on the block besides Miss Ada, Bonny, and Mr. Lester? Did anyone else depend upon him? Did he depend upon anyone else?
  d. Did Bill work for Miss Ada every afternoon?
  e. In what kind of jar did Bonny keep her pennies and dimes? Was it clear glass, colored glass, or opaque glass?

2. AWARENESS OF PROBLEM, DIFFICULTY, GAP IN KNOWLEDGE

Sometimes, it is a story in its entirety that makes the reader or listener aware of a problem. There are times when such awarenesses should be left until the story has been read and reflected upon. These awarenesses may come from the children themselves. They will come if there is freedom to ask questions, to want to know, and to make honest errors. At other times, the awareness of a problem may be created by a workbook exercise or by the teacher through questions and discussion. "You Can Depend on Bill" is one of those stories that might be presented so that the problem will not really burst into awareness until after the reading of the story has been completed—"why, Bill could be depended upon because he could depend on others!"

Awareness of gaps in information may send children to reference books, history books, geographies, to people, and to places. It takes only a bit of guidance and involvement on the part of the teacher and the children. Even in the primary grades, children are quite ready for such activities.

3. AWARENESS AND ACKNOWLEDGMENT OF PUPIL POTENTIALITY

Disadvantaged children seem to be virtually starved for someone to acknowledge some potentiality in them. Activities such as those sketched herein encourage all children to stretch their minds and exhibit many potentialities—for social responsibility, for human love and understanding, for reasoning, for thinking of ideas, for evaluating ideas, for creative writing, for making predictions, for acting, and for finding out things in various ways. All of these are manifestations of potentialities that need to be recognized and acknowledged by the teacher. It is only then that a truly alert and fully sensitive kind of guidance and direction can be given.

4. CONCERN ABOUT PROBLEMS HEIGHTENED

Heightening concern about a problem frequently requires that time be allowed for doing something about a problem, not just talking about it. If some freedom is being threatened, or if someone is not acting responsibly, this can be made the subject of involvement and action. One good way of developing such concern is to identify the concern as an outgrowth of reading the story and then to develop it through creative dramatics, role playing, writing letters, making speeches, creating posters, and the like, gradually digging more deeply into the concern and elaborating it.

5. CONSTRUCTIVE RESPONSE CALLED FOR (OTHER BETTER WAYS)

Once a concern has been aroused, as in 4 above, the matter should not be dropped. It should be reinforced by opportunity to think of and test better ways. Some of these, too, can be explored through creative dramatics, sociodrama, brainstorming, creative problem solving, and the like. I mean by this that the concern should be made the focus of group creative problem solving. In creative dramatics and sociodrama, the following steps should be followed:

a. Defining the problem
b. Establishing the situation (conflict)
c. Casting characters
d. Briefing and warming up the actors and observers
e. Acting out the situation or situations
f. Cutting the action

g. Discussing and analyzing behavior by actors and observers

h. Making plans for further testing of insights and for practicing the new behavior implied.

The testing of the new insights and behaviors can be practiced first in the role playing or sociodrama and then in the real situation. When encouragement is given for the practice of such behaviors in the classroom, at home, or in the community, the teacher should make it a practice to follow through by asking for reports and by giving guidance and direction in adopting new behavior, such as mutual interdependence. Efforts to learn the new behavior should be rewarding enough to "keep it going."

6. CONTINUITY WITH PREVIOUSLY LEARNED SKILLS, INFORMATION

Some of the suggestions given under "Building onto Existing Knowledge" in Chapter 7 can be expanded or picked up again after reading the story. Or, if these ideas were not used before the lesson, one of them could be introduced at this time. The teacher who really knows the children he teaches will have no difficulty in thinking of exercises that will build onto their existing knowledge and skills. Most disadvantaged children especially love learning new skills, and opportunities to teach them new skills should be used as frequently as possible. This gives them increased feelings of competence. They have to be warmed up to the task of learning new skills and be made to feel safe. They need success experiences so desperately that they will cling to old skills when there is threat of failure in learning new skills.

7. CREATIVE AND CONSTRUCTIVE ACCEPTANCE OF LIMITATIONS

When the curiosity and excitement of third grade children are aroused, it is impossible to provide them with all the resources and opportunities that they want in order to carry out their ideas. To teach the skills of creative and constructive rather than cynical acceptance of limitations, it is sometimes quite productive to limit the resources for accomplishing a task. For example, in the dramatization of a story, the class might be limited to certain props. In making a mural, the class might be limited to a certain space and to specific materials. For finding the information to fill the gaps, the class could be limited to certain sources. Their job would be to stretch their own abilities and to make the most of whatever resources are provided. This often brings about a kind of mind-stretching and creativity that does not occur when resources are relatively unlimited.

8. DIGGING MORE DEEPLY, GOING BENEATH THE OBVIOUS

"You Can Depend on Bill" provides many opportunities for encouraging children to go more deeply beyond the obvious. Several such possibilities have already been identified. The following are additional questions that identify some of these points and that might cause children to dig more deeply and go beyond the obvious or superficial:

a. Did Bill's efforts to hurry Bonny past Miss Ada's shop really have any effect on Bonny's dillydallying?
b. Did Bonny really want one of the dresses in Miss Ada's shop?
c. Did Bonny know how much one of Miss Ada's dresses cost?
d. Did Bonny know how much money she had saved in her jar?
e. Did Bill know how much money Bonny had saved?
f. Did Bonny's father want Bonny to have the fancy dress that Miss Ada made for her?
g. What would have happened if Bill had stolen a dress for Bonny from Miss Ada's shop?

9. Divergent Thinking Made Legitimate

Children are so accustomed to the one correct or best answer that they may be reluctant to think of other possibilities or to build up a pool of ideas to be evaluated later. It would be desirable if material to help make divergent thinking legitimate were to be inserted in reading textbooks, in skill practice books for pupils, and in teachers' editions. In accumulating a pool of ideas in group problem solving, it is usually a good idea to establish a rule to eliminate negative criticism. Guidance material in teachers' editions should from time to time emphasize the necessity for being respectful of divergent ideas rather than ridiculing them. The teacher should avoid stimulating divergent ideas unless he is willing to treat them with respect. This is extremely important with disadvantaged children, since they are especially fearful of and vulnerable to ridicule.

10. Elaborating upon What Is Read

The following are a few of the ways of elaborating "You Can Depend on Bill":

a. Draw a series of cartoons to tell the story.
b. Design and make a mural to recount the main incidents of the story.
c. Dramatize the story or some part of it.
d. Select music to serve as background for the reading or telling of the story.
e. Make puppets of the characters in the story and dramatize the story in a puppet theater.
f. With the music selected as background for the story, use the "Dance-a-Story" technique to produce physical involvement with the story as it is read.

g. Similarly, use mime theater techniques.

h. Write letters as though they were written by one of the characters of the story—Bill, Bonny, Mr. Lester, and Miss Ada. These
letters can describe the individual writer's private feelings as
he experienced the events of the story.

11. Elegant Solutions Encouraged

In trying to apply the idea of "the elegant solution" to a story such
as "You Can Depend on Bill," several approaches might be used. One
would be to distill the essence of the story in one picture, or in a new
title, a single theme, a symbol or abstract design, a short song or poem,
a motto, or the like. Another approach would be to try to find elegant
solutions to the central problem of the story, using the creative problem-
solving process. Since it deals with a developmental problem common
to almost all third graders, the children might be encouraged to think
of incidents in their own lives when someone expected something of
them that they could not do. An evaluation of the various events described by the members of a group will usually provide an "elegant
solution," the incident that would have the most elements common to
the story, "You Can Depend on Bill."

12. Empathic Metaphor to Give New Feeling
of Understanding

In order to produce a suitable metaphor, an exercise could be constructed to encourage the children to think of things in nature that
depend upon one another just as Bill, Bonny, Miss Ada, and Mr. Lester
depended upon one another. The following are a few examples, but third
grade children can probably think of better ones.

a. Legumes depend upon the soil for food, and they in turn put
nitrogen back into the soil.

b. Woodpeckers get their food by eating the insects on trees, and
this protects the trees from the insects.

c. Green algae in the cytoplasm of a sponge depend upon one
another, but algae may take over and become parasitic.

After a suitable analogy has been produced and selected, children can
imagine and act out how they would feel under various conditions if
they were one of these things. They could imagine that one member
of the pair has been attacked by an enemy and that the other helps to
save its life. Through movement and creative dramatics, they could
act out their feelings when trying to protect one another.

13. Experimentation Required

Several ideas for experimentation have already been given for "You
Can Depend on Bill." A directly relevant experiment would be for the

teacher to ask each child to do something beyond his power to do but which he can get someone else to do. The teacher tells him that he is depending on him. From this experience, much creative behavior should result, along with a more genuine understanding of the concept of responsibility and mutual interdependence.

14. FAMILIAR MADE STRANGE OR STRANGE MADE FAMILIAR

The ideas suggested under 12 and 13 above are also appropriate for making the strange familiar. The familiar could be made strange by comparing a common and familiar personal or classroom problem to the problem of the story.

15. FANTASIES EXAMINED TO FIND SOLUTIONS TO REALISTIC PROBLEMS

"You Can Depend on Bill" is not a fantasy but, like most fantasies, it may be used to help children deal with their own developmental problems. This can be done if they are given guidance in seeing similarities.

16. FUTURE PROJECTION ENCOURAGED

The story of "You Can Depend on Bill" may be presented as an incomplete story that could be followed by an assignment to complete the story in some way. The stories could be about Bonny as she runs back to the shoe repair shop to show her new dress to her father; her father as he follows Bill to the dress shop; Bonny as she wears her dress to church on Sunday or to a birthday party; Bonny and Bill as they come to their block after school the next day; or a life history of Bonny's dress. Projects might also include discussions, drawings of the grown-up Bill, dramatizations of Bill and his family in the future, and so forth.

17. GOING BEYOND WHAT IS READ

Properly managed, almost any of the exercises described in this section might take the reader beyond the textbook into other sources. The most straightforward application of this idea to "You Can Depend on Bill" would be to motivate reading about dressmaking, shoemaking, shoe repair, and the like.

18. IMPROBABILITIES ENTERTAINED

Third grade children will be able to think of many intriguing improbabilities or "just supposes" in connection with "You Can Depend on Bill." Here are a few examples:

    a. Just suppose Miss Ada sold nothing but little girls' dresses.

    b. Just suppose Bill had delivered a dress by mistake to Bonny instead of to the customer who was supposed to get it.

    c. Just suppose Mr. Lester had refused to repair Miss Ada's pumps.
    d. Just suppose Bill's mother would not let him have anything to do with Bonny and Mr. Lester just because they are black.
    e. Just suppose Mr. Lester refused to let Bill come into his store because Bill is not black.

19. Irrelevance Accepted and Used

The teacher can have the readers pick out things in the story and in the illustrations that seem to them to be irrelevant. The teacher could then show them how they really are relevant to the story and how the story would be different without them. Or, the teacher could ask the class to think of reasons why they are relevant.

20. Judgment Deferred

The importance of this characteristic has already been stressed in connection with several of the suggested exercises. From the available evidence, it seems that creative imagination and judgment cannot function concurrently at their highest level. And yet it is important that some criteria for judgment be established and that ideas be evaluated in terms of these criteria.

21. Knowledge from One Field Related to Knowledge from Another

The central idea of "You Can Depend on Bill" can be enriched from the social studies curriculum of the third grade and perhaps by other elements of the curriculum.

22. Looking at the Same Material in Different Ways

Suggestions for looking at the same material in different ways were made in Section A. Essentially, the same suggestions can be applied after the reading, perhaps with more profit.

23. Manipulation of Ideas and Objects Encouraged

Creative dramatics and the use of puppets are especially effective for encouraging the manipulation of ideas relevant to "You Can Depend on Bill." Through these media, a third grade class could explore a variety of ways that they can help others achieve the things they desire to achieve.

24. Multiple Hypotheses Encouraged

Any of the "Just Supposes" in 18 above would be good for developing skills of forming multiple hypotheses.

25. One Thing Permitted to Lead to Another

A reading activity may lead to other related reading activities, creative writing, art, dramatics, music, creative movement, history, economics, psychology, and the like.

26. Paradoxes Confronted and Examined

After the first reading of the story, children might be asked to reread the story in search of paradoxes. With third graders, it might be necessary to introduce and illustrate the concept of paradoxes. An example in "You Can Depend on Bill" would be Bonny's longing for dresses that were far too large for her, dresses that she could not possibly wear.

27. Play in Pushing a Scientific Law to Its Limits

Although this reading passage does not deal with scientific laws, the spirit of this characteristic can be applied. For example, what if two people depend upon one another too much? What would happen if a person tried to establish mutual interdependence with everyone he encounters? Let the children take one of these, step by step, and see how far they can go.

9

Finding Hidden Talents

Numerous scholars (Anderson, 1960; Riessman, 1962; Taba and Elkins, 1966) have written of the hidden talents among disadvantaged children. There has been a general recognition that existing methods of psychological assessment fail to discover these talents (Terman, 1925, 1954; Davis, 1948). Attempts to develop culture free (Cattell, 1949) and culture fair (Davis and Eells, 1953) tests of intellectual talent have not been very successful.

At the First Minnesota Conference on Gifted Children in 1958, John E. Anderson (1960) urged that we set up a searching procedure for identifying and utilizing talent throughout all socioeconomic levels. Somewhat later, Riessman (1962) proposed the category of the slow-gifted child among disadvantaged populations. Headstart programs have aimed at keeping alive some of those talents that "die young," and Upward Bound programs have attempted to rescue some of those talents that still show signs of life near the end of the high school period. In spite of these mammoth efforts, there have been no genuine breakthroughs in developing ways of finding hidden talents among disadvantaged children. Investigators (Bereiter and Englemann, 1966; Frost and Hawkes, 1966; Deutsch, 1967) have stuck to rather traditional assessment instruments and procedures.

In 1964, I proposed some test and non-test procedures for identifying creatively gifted children among economically and culturally disadvantaged groups. At that time, some evidence had accumulated to indicate that children from disadvantaged groups compare quite favorably with those from advantaged groups on the figural tests of creative thinking but not on the verbal tests (Torrance, 1963). Soon afterwards, Smith (1965) confirmed these findings. I knew that test procedures of all kinds would have to be supplemented by non-test indicators. Disadvantaged children are notoriously deficient in test-taking "know-how." In 1964, I had had little practical experience in

using non-test indicators of creative giftedness with disadvantaged children. The suggestions I offered at that time were, therefore, quite speculative, but I still believe that they would be useful.

Now that I have accumulated additional experience in the identification and development of creative talent among disadvantaged children, I would like to propose a general format and some specific techniques for procedures to discover hidden talents among disadvantaged children.

The Creativity Workshop Format

In the summers of 1967, 1968, and 1969, my students and I experimented with the general format of the creativity workshop for identifying and developing creative talent among disadvantaged children. These workshops were conducted in disadvantaged neighborhoods in Athens, Georgia. The 1967 workshop lasted for two weeks and enrolled about twenty-five children ranging in age from eight through twelve years, and the 1968 and 1969 ones lasted three weeks and enrolled sixty and fifty children respectively, varying in age from six through twelve years. Since there was no effective way of keeping other children away from the outdoor activities such as painting, creative movement, dramatics, and Hula Hoops, no one knows precisely how many children were involved in the 1968 workshop.

The program featured each day some large group, small group, and individual creative activity. Drawing, painting, dramatics, dancing, storytelling, singing, puppetry, creative problem solving, sociodrama, and photography were featured. During the process, each child was administered the *Torrance Tests of Creative Thinking* (Torrance, 1966) according to new procedures to be described later. During the final week, a large proportion of the time was devoted to work in specialization groups in which the children were encouraged strongly to try to excel in at least one activity. A second emphasis was on seeing beautiful things in the immediate environment and in making them more beautiful. A third emphasis was on the development of creative problem-solving skills through the solution of group and community problems. Throughout the workshop, each child was assigned a sponsor or "special teacher," a member of my class on "Learning Problems of Disadvantaged Children." In 1968, the small community center which housed the workshop was reserved for the younger children in the mornings and for the older children in the afternoons. In 1969, the facilities of a city park in a low-income neighborhood were used.

In these settings, we hoped to become aware of both the learning problems and the creative potentialities of these disadvantaged children.

The overall rationale of the Creativity Workshop as a format for finding hidden talents among disadvantaged children is based on the simple assumption that no talents will be found unless their possessors are motivated to exercise them. No one would think of trying to discover jumping ability by observing how high people just happen to jump. Neither would anyone try to identify jumping ability without giving the jumpers a chance to become warmed up. The same principles apply to the identification of creative thinking abilities, as well as other intellectual abilities. In fact, problems of motivation are more serious in the measurement of intelligence than is usually recognized and acknowledged. For example, Ronald Goldman (Torrance, 1965c) found that a group of adolescents in a teen-age club scored an average of 25 I.Q. points higher than they had scored in school. In school, they had not been motivated to behave intelligently; in the club, they had been motivated to exercise their intelligence.

In the Creativity Workshops, extensive attempts were made to motivate creative behavior, and many strategies were used to facilitate the warm-up process. A few of the more promising procedures will be described.

Tests of Creative-Thinking Ability

In the format of the Creativity Workshop, tests of creative-thinking ability take on more power to discover hidden talents among disadvantaged children than in typical situations. Even in formal situations, disadvantaged children perform rather well on the figural tests of creative-thinking ability (Torrance, 1967a). Their performance on the verbal tests, however, is quite poor in the formal school situation. This is, of course, in line with numerous findings concerning the generally poor performance of disadvantaged children on almost all kinds of verbal tasks and on speeded or timed tests.

In the Creativity Workshop, three procedures were used to elicit the hidden verbal abilities for which we were searching. No tests were given until there had been time for the creative processes of the children to become warmed up. No time limits were imposed. The examiners offered to record the children's ideas. These procedures were generally quite effective. No one observing these activities could have said that these children were nonverbal.

Several unanticipated difficulties arose, however. Some children expressed awe and fear of the test booklet. We were reminded of the observation of Taba and Elkins (1966) that tests cause pandemonium among disadvantaged children. They reported that disadvantaged youngsters would take one look at a test and scream, "I can't do it. Ten pages!" and that some would weep, yell, or rush from the room to return no more that day. This behavior is in contrast with that of some kindergarteners who delight in filling up a book.

Some children would enter into the verbal tests with great energy only to complain that they were fatigued after completing two or three of the seven activities. In such cases, we discontinued the testing and returned to it on the following day. In a typical school situation, this fatigue would probably go unnoticed, and the examiner would be amazed at the lack of responsiveness and the apparent paralysis of verbal creative-thinking ability. Fatigue among disadvantaged children on such tests is quite understandable. All-out performance on the first two or three tasks took a great deal of expensive energy. Furthermore, many of them came in the afternoons without any lunch and/or breakfast.

The open-ended nature of the verbal tests of creative thinking are excellently suited to disadvantaged children. Since there are no single correct answers, children can respond at their own level and in the context of their own experiences and culture.

Creative Dramatics

Numerous investigators have reported that disadvantaged children are articulate in role playing and creative dramatics. Since drama calls for problem solving and has good warm-up qualities, creative dramatics seemed a natural vehicle for searching for hidden talents. In most respects, our expectations were realized. One student, a school social worker, made the following observation:

> Most disadvantaged children appear non-verbal when confronted with intellectual tasks but will readily ventilate their feelings when asked to play a role or to dramatize something. In this way, they can put things in their own words and in the context of their experiences. This is a very meaningful concept I learned in the Workshop. I expect to use it in social group work.

Many of the children in our Workshop exhibited strong feelings of fear and either refused to attempt roles or were unable to play roles with gusto. One device used to cope with this difficulty was the "Magic Net" described in Chapter 1. The following comment by one student describes the general reaction to this technique:

> The Magic Net became our creator of another saga of princesses— this time including bullfighters and a hummingbird . . . The children all seemed to like the magical touch of the net with power to help them become anything they wished. They also found the net a source of security when all eyes were upon them.

An interesting characteristic found among both the younger and the older children was the tendency to choose the same role that their peers had chosen. If one girl chose to be a queen, all the girls would choose to be queens, and the boys would choose to be kings. They seemed to have a strong need for the support of their peers, for the co-experiencing of roles. Consequently, it became necessary to create stories with five queens and five kings, or with five witches and five old men. Even when a child chose a unique role, it was sometimes necessary to reinforce him with other children in the same role.

In the 1969 workshop, the beautiful outdoor setting of a city park almost surrounded by a little river provided new possibilities in creative dramatics. One of the most interesting plays staged by the puppeteers was one in which the puppets played outdoors on the slides, the merry-go-round, and the other playground equipment. The following report by one of the creative dramatics directors illustrates how the outdoor setting can stimulate creative behavior:

> As soon as we met, Isanay shyly announced that she had read "The Three Billy Goats Gruff" . . . It was obvious that she was interested in acting out her story. She did so much better than at any previous time . . . She immediately claimed the role of the troll. Since this story involves a bridge under which the troll lives, we decided to use the footbridge at the lower end of the park. The children decided that since the bridge was public property, the troll had no right to deny access to anyone who wanted to use it. So instead of having the big billy goat gruff commit mayhem on the troll, they arrested the troll and carted him away to jail to be tried by a judge and jury. There was definite improvement in participation. Every one of them spoke up so that he could be heard, and they really seemed to be having fun doing this play . . . Today we read them a play. They didn't seem interested. They definitely get more out of creating their own "thing" or giving a new interpretation of a familiar story.

Creative Writing

Somewhat surprisingly, creative writing proved to be an excellent vehicle for revealing hidden talents in the Creativity Workshop. In the announcement of the Workshop, creative writing had been listed as one of the activities. Reportedly, the common response upon reading this was either, "Ugh!" or "Not me!" Thus, I knew that successful experiences in creative writing would require some unusual kind of encouragement. Our two most successful devices proved to be puppetry and the imaginative reading of stories.

Perhaps the most successful storytelling experience was my own rendition of *The Red Balloon* (Lamorisse, 1956). One student wrote the following comment concerning this experience:

> The fantasy of *The Red Balloon* intrigued the children. There have been few times when they have been so quiet, involved, and attentive. If the stimulus is powerful and meaningful, they will re-

main attentive and disprove all theories regarding the notorious "short attention span" of disadvantaged children. Another characteristic brought out vividly was the lack of control (delay of gratification) of behavior when a reward is ensuing. When the additional balloons were brought out to illustrate the mass of balloons that assembled to take the little boy around the world after "The Red Balloon" had been killed, there was virtually no restraint . . .

After the "Magic Net" had been applied to calm them down and "replace greed with love," each child was motivated to tell a story about the trip with the magic balloons. One student described her observations of her protégée's response as follows:

> Delores did want to see more and know more today. The magic balloon helped her put into words what she wanted to see and do, and also what she wanted to be. It helped her get rid of some of her inhibitions for a short while and live in a dream world and tell a story about it.

Another summarized his observations of the puppetry group as follows:

> Of the many traits displayed in the puppet group, these seemed to be the most outstanding. They were witty, imaginative, artistic, alert, humorous, persistent, talkative, musical, intelligent, and creative.

The creation of cinquains involving the brainstorming process described in Chapter 8 also proved to be quite successful in putting creativity into the children's writing and in evoking emotional response. Some elements of this experience are reported by one of the creative-writing teachers in the following excerpt:

> I have been completely amazed by the interest the girls have shown in cinquains. We introduced them on Friday . . . They were fascinated and even worked a little over the weekend on it. This interest was surprising because we had difficulty evoking conventional writing from them even though we tried many ideas. Obviously, they were not motivated to write the conventional things.
>
> In their writing cinquains, I also discovered that their language contains rich imagery. Their terminology is frequently unique and sometimes nice. To describe the other creative-writing teacher, Grace said that he has a "king nose."

With the younger children, some of the creative-writing teachers found that a physical warm-up or an observation experience opened them up to composing cinquains and to other language arts experiences. One such experience is described in the following excerpt.

> Cassandra commented on the color of the water—muddy, dirty, polluted . . . the current—slow, swift, made circles, pushes leaves along . . . you can make shadows in the water by bending your fingers over it—it's a fun game . . . we hear buzzing, chirping, whist-

ling, croaking . . . no matter how stagnant, the water is full of life
. . . such pretty flowers and greenery around the water . . . Cas-
sandra just opened up, to my amazement, because I believe her
speech impediment made her unconfident. Her questions and answers were self-motivated and were sheer poetry.

Creative Music

Music and dance seemed to be natural media for learning for most
of the disadvantaged children in our three workshops, particularly the
one in 1969. The following excerpt from the creative-music teacher's
report illustrates how music may be used to encourage creative skills
outside of music itself:

> In our music activity today, I learned that small children are
> naturally curious. The older children have not shown such curiosity.
> Something must kill that curiosity as they grow older. These small
> children were very much interested in the theory of the flutes which
> they heard Barbara and Cynthia play. Even hyperactive Tammy was
> quiet. Little fat Mark began the series of questions *about* the flute.
> He asked me to tell about the holes in the flute. I saw how inter-
> ested they were and dropped my lesson plans and began to nurture
> that interest . . . All this interest in theory came as a total shock to
> me. I had no idea in the world that these children would be inter-
> ested or had the attention span to listen that long about abstracts . . .
> I believe that teaching is best done when interest is high. I do not
> believe in forcing information on a child, especially if it is irrelevant
> to him. It is my responsibility to make the information relate to him
> and to present it to him so that he will want it.

The creative music teacher had thought that the boys would shy
away from the music activity. To her surprise, she found that many of
them were more enthusiastic than the girls. They were particularly
fond of some of the mini-operas that they produced. One of the most
popular sessions was a kind of original version of *Pagliacci* which gave
the boys made up as clowns a chance to demonstrate their tumbling
and fighting skills.

Psychomotor Skills

The psychomotor skills involved in Hula Hoops and Frisbees provided especially good vehicles for helping the children work through
some of their blocks to learning and move on to creative performances.
Although competition was not emphasized, the demands of a contest
proved to be useful in helping some of them move from familiar skills in
which they were expert, to new skills, and thence to creative skills. One
of the Hula Hoop directors describes a part of this process in the following excerpt:

> Their emphasis on the familiar caused some children problems
> today. In the Hula Hoop contest, it was necessary to ask the chil-

dren to do as many tricks as possible to get a winner. This involved asking some children to do tricks they were not very good at doing, and several refused even to try but wanted to stay with what they did well. I took as much time as I could to explain why I had asked them to do these other tricks, and usually they would comply. However, it was obvious that they wanted to continue doing the tricks they had learned well and not any others.

One of the instructors describes another aspect of the process in the following report:

> Today I became aware of what seems to be a major key to creativity in doing physical skills. The children have been working very hard on the basic skills of the Hula Hoop and, in general, they are becoming very good in the performance of these skills. My observations seem to tell me that there is a direct correlation between how well the child can perform and how many original tricks he can think of and perform. It seems that when he does not have to concentrate on every movement he can then direct his attention toward creating his own skills. When these children finally got a trick down and then invented one of their own, their excitement gave me a feeling of accomplishment that I have never had before when working with children.

At every hand, the teachers found that the fear of failure was a great inhibitor of learning, and some found that turning away at times freed the children to try new skills, as expressed in the following report of a Hula Hoop instructor:

> Some of the children were too shy to try doing a trick with the Hula Hoop when I asked them to. But if I left them for a short while, when I looked back, they would be doing what I had asked of them. I think they were afraid of failure before an audience . . . They developed different ways of doing the same trick and enjoyed trying something different.

The teachers also discovered, however, that there were other times when having someone to look at a performance was the really powerful motivating force, as another instructor reported:

> When reading research on the disadvantaged children and how they desire someone to love them, it is just someone's study; but when you are actually working with them, it is obvious. Time after time, certain ones will wait until we are looking at them before they throw the Frisbee just to hear us say, "Very good, Willie." And when there is a chance, the young boys will pass by and reach out and touch us. To see their eyes brighten and their warm response to your sharing these moments together is very rewarding to the children and me.

Intellectual and Social Skills

In the 1969 workshop, intellectual and social skills seemed to be just as exciting as physical, artistic, and musical skills. The increased

confidence and feeling of competence that seemed to come with the
acquisition of skills provided powerful motivation. One day during the
skills-learning during the second half of the morning, one of the teachers
from the first session observed several of the groups and reported her
impressions as follows:

> As I moved from group to group, I realized more and more
> that this type of learning belongs in the public schools! I noticed
> how much Mark enjoyed building houses with blocks. Two girls
> were having fun learning to stitch or "paint with embroidery."

The teachers, however, had a few lessons to learn about teaching
skills, as reflected in the following comment by an excellent experienced
teacher:

> I noticed that when I told Leatha the word for the skill I was
> to teach her, "weaving," she more or less tuned me out. I found she
> did not have any idea what the word "weaving" meant. She showed
> no curiosity at all. I could get her interested only by demonstrating
> the process. When she saw the result, she was very eager to try.

The teachers learned, however, that skills mastery is itself motivating and will impel the learner forward, as expressed in the following
excerpt:

> One creative positive in today's work was the fact that a child
> will, by himself, go to other skills involving the ones already mastered
> if he is helped to enjoy the activity. This should be an incentive to
> the teacher continually to be aware and be prepared to introduce
> the new skills before he loses the student.

Teachers found that the learning of many skills, such as the skills
required to play games like checkers, could be used as the vehicle for
teaching an intellectual skill like, for example, causal thinking:

> We decided to play checkers during our individual skills period.
> I observed one distinct characteristic displayed in James' movement
> of the checkers, and this was the cause and effect of a move made
> by him. He would not observe movements by me and countered with
> movements to stop me. He knew how to play, but the cause and
> effect of a move of one checker on the others had no meaning to
> him. I shall pursue this skill on Friday during our session.

Small Group Creative Problem Solving

Each year, we were constantly amazed at how much more effectively disadvantaged children functioned in small groups of four or
five than they did either individually or in large groups (twenty to
thirty). In small groups, they showed less regressive behavior, produced
more imaginative ideas, and exercised better judgment. With some guidance from an adult in each group, the children were able to perform

successfully and with enjoyment all the steps in the creative problem-solving process as described by Parnes (1967). After one creative problem-solving session on broken Hula Hoops, one teacher wrote the following comment:

> When the "dead" (broken) Hula Hoop was presented, it caught the attention of the children, and they were ready to produce ideas because it was something vital and related to them. They were also offered a prize, an incentive which doubled their interest and involvement . . .

Although many educators object to the use of prizes to motivate creative thinking, their use seemed justified in the Creativity Workshops. First, it seemed to be one acceptable way of putting play facilities into a disadvantaged neighborhood seriously lacking them. Furthermore, their use seemed to produce very decided changes among some children. The following comment, written by a teacher, describes one such change:

> I learned today that Gwendolyn can be just as ebullient as any other child. When her group won the contest to produce ideas on "dead Hula Hoops" and she become the recipient of a Hula Hoop, I have never seen such a metamorphosis! Her eyes lit up—she trembled with excitement as she went for her prize. This was one time when she seemed to have few inhibitions. I received another thrill when Gwendolyn decided to join our singing group and learned the three verses of the song in a short time. She even showed her prowess today with a Hula Hoop. She really burgeoned!

Teaching the skills of creative problem-solving was a new experience for almost all the experienced teachers participating in the workshop. The following evaluations by some of them reflect some of the potentialities of this learning approach in finding the hidden talents of disadvantaged children:

> I was pleased and surprised to see children contributing to the idea-gathering process in such an uninhibited way when these same children only last week seemed too shy and unsure of themselves even to speak. This is most encouraging and satisfying to me personally.
>
> I arrived at this positive conclusion today that brainstorming is a most useful device for "bringing out" the creative potential that disadvantaged children have. Simple observation and "before and after" comparisons make this obvious.
>
> I was able to work with a small group of three in the problem solving. The most obvious thing to me was their ability to consider something in a very serious manner. Today, by using certain criteria, we judged the ideas the boys had suggested. These children did not take this matter lightly as some children might have done. They were serious and tried to consider every possible factor.

I learned that enthusiasm is contagious. I could hardly stay in my seat on the sidelines during the brainstorming. If we went back to our schools and did these things openly (almost like advertising), other *good* teachers would become enthusiastic and try. I liked the gradual building up to the fast pace during the brainstorming. I wonder what would have happened if the children were taken fast from the very beginning.

Creative Positives of Disadvantaged Children

From the workshops and other experiences with disadvantaged children, I have formulated what I consider the creative positives of disadvantaged children. I contend that it will not be possible to find hidden talents among disadvantaged children as long as we insist on identifying only those kinds of talent that will persist and lead to outstanding success in spite of the toughest kinds of deprivation, degradation, and discouragement. We shall also fail as long as we are interested only in those kinds of talent that the dominant, advantaged culture values. We must also look for and cultivate talents of the type that are valued in the various disadvantaged subcultures of our country.

My position is that not only should we identify and cultivate the talents valued by a particular subculture, but that we shall be more successful if we do. Criticisms of our established talent assessment procedures when applied to disadvantaged children and youth are too well known to be enumerated. On the positive side, we can point with some degree of success in the identification and cultivation of talent among disadvantaged groups in instrumental and vocal music, dancing, dramatics, visual art, and athletics. Even here, there has been gross neglect of talent. There has always been far more of this kind of talent than we have been willing to recognize and use.

I have offered two suggestions for finding hidden talent among disadvantaged children, and my colleague, Kay Bruch, has offered a third. It seems to me that a part of the difficulty, but only a part of it, lies in the nature of the talent tests, whatever their nature. Most of them require that the child respond in terms of the experiences common in our dominant, advantaged culture. The disadvantaged child is not permitted to respond in terms of his own experiences, the experiences common in his culture or unique to himself. Most tests of creativity—and the *Torrance Tests of Creative Thinking* (Torrance, 1966) in particular—permit disadvantaged children to respond in terms of their own experiences. This increases the chances of obtaining responses and makes it possible to evaluate the responses in terms of the child's experiences, whatever they might be.

Other problems of talent identification are almost completely outside the nature of the instruments used in the process. In order to obtain an indication of potentiality from a child, it is necessary to motivate him to display that potentiality and to feel psychologically safe in doing so. We must continue to search for test administration procedures that are practical, and yet that achieve results similar to the creativity workshop format.

Kay Bruch (1969) has made another important point. She contends that, for the disadvantaged, the identification question cannot be whether they perform on tests of intelligence or achievement at a currently high level, but whether there are indices of probable development to higher levels than those at which they now function. She offers as an example a youth who had demonstrated exceptional talent in music, a culturally valued talent among the black disadvantaged. She argues that this youth may also be able to function more fully through latent abilities in academic areas. She suggests that through his specific culturally valued talent, music, a developmental program could be built for the needed abilities in vocabulary fluency and comprehension, mathematical symbolic thinking, and other thinking processes.

I believe that the following six creative positives of disadvantaged children occur to a high degree among them and can be used as the basis for successful educational programs for them:

1. *High Non-Verbal Fluency and Originality.* On the figural forms of the *Torrance Tests of Creative Thinking* (1966), disadvantaged groups almost always hold their own or even excel similar advantaged groups. This seems to hold true in a variety of localities throughout the United States and for Negroes, American Indians, Mexican-Americans, and Caucasians.

2. *High Creative Productivity in Small Groups.* In my experience, I have found disadvantaged children to be more highly productive in small groups than as individuals or in large group situations. They even become quite verbal in small group creative problem-solving situations and seem less inhibited than more advantaged children.

3. *Adeptness in Visual Art Activities.* In every disadvantaged group with which I have worked, there have been surprisingly large numbers of gifted artists. In some cases, they have persisted in being copyists rather than trust their own originality. They become more imaginative and inventive as they become involved in group activities such as puppetry, making large paintings, and the like.

4. *High Creativity in Movement, Dance, and Other Physical Activities.* Disadvantaged children seem to take naturally to work in creative movement, dance, and other physical activities. Many of them will work hard at these activities and develop considerable discipline. Two

of the girls in our 1968 workshop won district Hula Hoop champion-
ships, and one of them later won the city championship and was second
place winner in the state contest. In 1969, Hula Hoops and Frisbees
again proved to be activities through which children developed discipline and achieved considerable success.

5. *High Motivation by Games, Music, Sports, Humor, and Concrete Objects.* The warm-up effects of games, music, sports, humor,
and the like seem to enable disadvantaged children to achieve a higher
level of mental functioning than otherwise attained. Success in these
activities gives us something on which to build other skills and competencies.

6. *Language Rich in Imagery.* In telling stories, making up songs,
spontaneously enacting dramas, and producing solutions to problems,
disadvantaged children's language is rich in imagery.

These six characteristics I would like to call the "Creative Positives
of Disadvantaged Children." I believe that it is upon these positives
that we can and must build educational programs for "the unrecognized
and unawakened potential of disadvantaged children."

10

Awakening
Unrecognized Potential

Almost anyone who reads some of the realistic and intimate published accounts of teachers who work with children who live in poverty comes away with a feeling of hopelessness. This is especially true of experiences in reading Bel Kaufman's *Up the Down Staircase* (1964), Robert Kendall's *White Teacher in a Black School* (1964), Elizabeth M. Eddy's *Walk the White Line* (1965), James Herndon's *The Way It Spozed to Be* (1965), Margaret Anderson's *The Children of the South* (1966), Jonathan Kozol's *Death at an Early Age* (1967), Herbert Kohl's *36 Children* (1967), and Robert Coles' *Dead End School* (1968). Even though I fear that the picture presented by these books is fairly accurate insofar as the great bulk of the education of disadvantaged children is concerned, I still believe that it is possible to awaken through creative development the unrecognized and unawakened potentialities of disadvantaged children.

One finds some hope for awakening the creative potentialities of disadvantaged children in books such as E. R. Braithwaite's *To Sir, with Love* (1959), Robert Rosenthal and Lenore Jacobson's *Pygmalion in the Classroom* (1968), and William Glasser's *Schools without Failure* (1969). In none of these books were any deliberate efforts made to make use of our new understandings of creative motivations, and yet we find faint traces that there were creative awakenings in all three of these projects. Braithwaite (1959), a black teacher in a predominantly white school in England, brought about intellectual, emotional, and creative awakenings among his students through a kind, firm, stimulating approach to teaching and an original program for building upon the few learning skills that these adolescents had attained. Rosenthal and Jacobson (1968) found large gains in intelligence among Mexican-American children whose teachers had been told that these particular children (randomly chosen) were expected to show spurts of intellectual development. Their study, though highly criticized by some people,

suggests that children's development is influenced markedly by the expectations that teachers have of them. Glasser (1969) seems to have accomplished remarkable results in schools in poverty areas through a program featuring classroom meetings and emphases on helping children find success in some important area of their lives and in developing social responsibility.

Again, I believe that we are doomed to failure in awakening this unrecognized potential as long as we insist upon holding onto schools characterized by instruction in fixed groupings called "classes," the use of the "classroom" as the principal or only facility, and the progression of the student by annual "grade" steps. I agree with many of the ideas of Leslie Hart's *The Classroom Disaster* which maintains that this system of education has become a brutal, inhuman means of inflicting on our children planned restriction, suppression, discouragement, frustration, upside-down values, and humiliation (1969).

I must admit that I know of no large-scale, institutionally sanctioned experiment in which a school system has departed from these traditions to facilitate the creative development of this unrecognized and unawakened potential among disadvantaged children. Many of the teachers who have tried hardest to awaken this potential have admitted that what they tried to get to happen actually happened in the hallways or on the playground during recess.

I would like to tell you briefly about three small but successful programs through which unrecognized and unawakened potentialities among disadvantaged children flowered in learning situations outside of the traditional classroom system. The setting for one was a ghetto area in New Haven, Connecticut. For the second, the setting was Fernwood, a poverty area near Portland, Oregon. The third setting was a Baltimore slum.

The New Haven Experiment

Four summers ago, George Witt (1968), a school psychologist, initiated the New Haven experiment and has given it continuity to this date. It is called the Life Enrichment Activity Program and was initiated for a group of sixteen highly creative, lower class Negro children in a ghetto setting. He believed that highly creative children are injured more in such settings than are their less creative peers. Witt selected his sixteen highly creative children from the second through fourth grade of a ghetto school solely on the basis of tests of creative thinking (*The Torrance Tests of Creative Thinking* and one test task that Witt himself devised).

Twelve of the original sixteen children have continued in the program for over three years, and all of them have manifested high level creative skills in fields such as music, art, science, and writing. Much work has been done with the families of these boys. In many instances, the highly creative talents of siblings have been recognized, and opportunities have been provided for them to have music, art, ballet, and other kinds of lessons from outstanding teachers. In a few instances, it has been possible to help the parents of the children upgrade their own job skills and acquire better jobs.

In fashioning a program for highly creative, inner city children, Witt attempted to incorporate the following major characteristics:

1. be clearly structured but flexible;
2. provide for opportunities to be rewarded for solving problems;
3. be viewed by one and all in a positive light;
4. be tangible; and have many activities conducted in the homes;
5. have enough competent adults in charge to minimize the need for the ubiquitous instant jeering and quarreling;
6. continue controls indefinitely;
7. involve exciting people from the inner and non-inner city;
8. design all learning experiences so that exciting perceptual-motor experiences precede, accompany, and follow cognitive growth;
9. be intimately coordinated by a director expert in individual, group, and community dynamics;
10. provide for the support, control, and involvement of the children's families, parents, and siblings.

Each year, Witt reports, new structural elements have been added to the program as the children, their families, and the programs have grown.

During the first part of the program, the specialists who worked with the program began to doubt that the children who had been selected had any kind of creative potentialities. Witt encouraged them to keep working, however, and he continued working with the children and involving their families. Before the end of the first summer, all the children had exhibited outstanding promise in at least one creative field, and many of them had shown unusual promise in two or more areas.

It would be hazardous to predict the adult futures of the twelve children who have continued in the program devised by Witt and called "LEAP" (Life Enrichment Activity Program). The present indications, however, are that these children are developing talents that are highly valued both in their own subcultures and in the dominant culture, that their families are supporting their development and, in most cases, developing along with them. There are indications that such talents can be identified at least as early as age eight and that there is a bountiful supply of such talent in almost all disadvantaged groups.

Initially, Witt had conceived of the creative activities as a side-line or as "the frosting on the cake." Very soon, these activities—art, creative writing, dramatics, music, dancing, and the like—became the real meat of the program. Other things failed. These were the things in which the children could succeed and upon which they could build other skills, concepts, and competencies. Consequently, this program was essentially both beyond the classroom and beyond the curriculum.

The Fernwood Experiment

The Fernwood experiment was conceived and directed by Elizabeth Drews (1968). The area where the children lived is one of great natural beauty, although most of the houses are shabby and many of the residents impoverished. Wild flowers, ferns and shrubs, many bird species, wild animals, and towering Douglas firs invited the budding biologists, naturalists, and ecologists in the experiment to look and listen carefully and sometimes to study in depth. Drews explains that ordinarily the youngsters did none of these things. They knew little or nothing of nature, watched TV instead of birds, and were generally unaware of the intellectual and aesthetic possibilities of the natural world around them. Many of these children had little space to claim as their own beyond a spot in bed.

In this Oregon experiment, twenty-four pupils were randomly selected from grades 7, 8, and 9. Two very capable teacher-counselors told these young people as they sat in their bare classroom that they could make theirs the kind of school they wanted. "They could find out what was important to them and then work on what was important." The arrangement of the room and what it was to contain was up to them. Since the experiment began in September, the out-of-school environment proved to be irresistible. When the pupils realized that they were really free to choose, they revelled in it. Only one or two of them would sit through even the most dynamic lectures prepared by the teachers. In the free environment of Fernwood, they sought out personal refuges, sometimes in groups, but often singly.

The most confirmed low achiever and general misfit, according to Drews, was a boy of sixteen—a non-reader with a tested I.Q. that placed him in the moron category. He was generally belligerent and was mean to the younger children. He had been thrown out of school repeatedly and had come back more resistant to learning each time. He had been an habitual truant, but his attendance at Fernwood was perfect. At first, he spent all his time outdoors. Gradually, he gained enough peace of mind so that he overcame his aversion to school and could enter the classroom. Then, as Drews wrote, "By dint of alchemy or miracle (and perhaps with the aid of a stack of 200 plus or minus comic books) he learned to read." Next he began to become social. He learned to play chess, occasionally winning the game over his teachers. By the time the experiment was abandoned in December because of cancellation of funds, he had become an excellent conversationalist who could talk about war and peace as well as the vagaries of the weather. A year after the program ended, he was spending half of each day helping mentally retarded children in a special room, and he is known for his gentleness and loving ways.

At Fernwood, there was time to listen to music, to build things, to plan and go on trips, to read books and talk about them, and to form natural and meaningful interpersonal relationships. At home, these youngsters had usually been engaged in endless chores. At school, relentless bells had dictated when their minds were to be turned on and off and what words their eyes were to focus upon. The curriculum was text-centered and fact-oriented. Talk, except in recitations, was regarded as idle chatter, discouraged in the classrooms, and forbidden in the halls. At Fernwood, there was freedom to dream and envision what one might be and become. The warmth and trust of the teachers finally won over the more reluctant children.

Many exciting things occurred during Fernwood's four-month existence. A non-reader began to read without pressure of applied methods and scheduled class periods. Those who had habitually failed English discovered that they could speak fluently and well when they could talk about something of interest. A boy who had been indifferent to mathematics did four months of work in mathematics within three days and ended up six weeks ahead of his former classmates. The youngsters became aware of changes in themselves and, near the end of the term, commented that they had not destroyed property of Fernwood—not even those children who had been the most hardened marauders. One of them said, "I was not closed in at Fernwood, I wasn't in a cage or cell, so I didn't need to destroy." These pupils did not "lose ground" by being out of the regular school program for four months. All except two of them did better work and received higher grades upon their return to school than they had done prior to the free experience.

Free to learn in their own ways about things that they wanted to know, the pupils made almost all the suggestions of things to do. Some of them became so addicted to reading that parents complained. Four girls decided to go to England to widen their horizon, and they searched diligently but in vain for jobs for fourteen-year-olds. They decided to become columnists and began writing a teen-age column which they sold to the local paper. Later, the publisher of a teen-age paper "discovered" their talent, and one of the girls was asked to become his editor. Only history will reveal what else is yet to come from this bold, but short-lived experiment.

A Poetry Project in a Baltimore Slum

Another interesting ray of hope comes from an unlikely poetry project conducted in a vocational-technical school in the inner city area of Baltimore by students of Goucher College (Howe, 1969). Let me tell you a bit about the Baltimore project, because I think it demonstrates how creativity development can awaken unrecognized potentialities under what would appear to be very improbable situations. The Goucher undergraduates had not been trained as teachers, but they knew and loved poetry, and they knew about "open questions" that provoke deep, creative thinking about poetry. Their pupils were tenth grade boys in the auto mechanics curriculum. The school faculty was quite skeptical as to what would happen with untrained teachers.

The teaching was in small groups of five or six boys. The poems selected by the Goucher girls ranged from very brief "pop" poetry to a relatively long narrative poem by Robert Frost called "Out, Out." They taught the boys about open and closed questions and told them that they did not have to play the traditional game of closed, single answer questions. As the boys discovered that they could actually determine curriculum, they became less shy about saying what they liked. They enjoyed solving the puzzle posed by some of the poems. They liked poems that were difficult but not too difficult. They thought that a poem had to have "something to say." There were serious discussions about matters such as the way the boys lived, and about race, policemen, drugs, war, religion, and so forth.

How can we evaluate such experiences? How do we know that such creative experiences awakened unrecognized potentialities? The project participants had several discussions concerning what method they could use to get an evaluation without testing the pupils. Finally, they decided to give the boys four poems that they had not previously seen. The boys were asked to write about one of the four poems that they particularly liked and to explain why they did and what the poem was saying. Most of them wrote freely, assured that their papers would not be corrected or graded. One of the school's regular teachers who had been skeptical all along conducted her own experiment. She gave the same writing assignment to other classes in the school which had not had this kind of creative experience with poetry. She admitted that, by any standards, the boys taught by the Goucher students were superior to the others. This may sound like a miracle, but it isn't. I do not think that this experience tells us that teachers do not need to learn methods. They do. I think the Goucher undergraduates had learned some good methods. They knew the method of open-end questions. They understood that poems communicate feelings and that the teacher's method must help pupils get to the poem's words by encouraging and permit-

ting open response to feelings. Even when we do not share ideas or
values, we share feelings. We also share the language of feelings—
sadness, joy, suffering, anger, wonder. Perhaps this is a way into language for deprived children and for young people who are labeled as
non-verbal.

What Else Is Needed?

In stressing the importance of creativity development to awaken
unrecognized potential, I must make it crystal clear that I do not see
it as a panacea or cure-all. We all know that much else is necessary.
Certainly, we must see that basic physiological and psychological needs
are satisfied. Unrecognized potential will not be awakened among children and young people who are hungry, cold, inadequately clothed and
housed—among children whose lives are unsafe—who feel that they do
not belong—whose dignity is not respected—who experience no love,
respect, or self-esteem. If this unrecognized potential is to be awakened,
children must be supplied with what Maslow (1968) calls B-values—
love, truth, beauty, and justice. Maslow points out the well-known
fact that taking away all love from children can kill them. Children
need truth in the same way. The child deprived of truth becomes para-
noid, mistrusting everybody, searching for hidden meanings. Deprivation
of beauty also causes illness. Children become very much depressed and
uncomfortable in ugly surroundings. It affects their whole being—memory, thinking, creativity, judgment. Deprivation of justice also sickens,
and history tells what happens to people deprived of justice for a long
time.

For unrecognized potential to become awakened, there must be
a feeling of purpose—a feeling of destiny. Some Hippies in California
told me that I am too achievement-oriented in my thinking about creativity. Perhaps I am, but I have always insisted upon the importance
of the intrinsic motivation inherent in creative ways of learning and
in creative activities. Extrinsic motivations may be effective in many
instances, but both reward and punishment are quite erratic in their
effects. Even when they are effective, they must be applied again and
again to keep learning going. Maslow (1968) tells the amusing anecdote
of a psychology class that played a prank on their professor by secretly
conditioning him while he was delivering a lecture on conditioning.
The professor, without realizing it, began nodding more and more. By
the end of the lecture, he was nodding continually. As soon as the class
told the professor what he was doing, he stopped nodding. After that,
no amount of smiling on the part of the class could make him nod again.
Truth had made the learning disappear. The very essence of creativity

development is the search for truth. Such learning is enduring, and there is built-in motivation that keeps the process going.

Among other things, love, truth, beauty, and justice will encourage creativity among disadvantaged children and the unrecognized and unawakened potentialities among them. I also believe that the procedures for encouraging creativity presented in this book are especially well-suited to the purpose of awakening unrecognized potentialities among disadvantaged children.

Appendix A

Ideal Child Checklist

To guide a child to the highest fulfillment of his potentialities, what characteristics or behaviors should be encouraged and discouraged? Indicate your ideas, using the list below: (1) Check (✔) each characteristic or behavior that you think should be encouraged; (2) double-check (✔✔) each characteristic or behavior that you think should be especially encouraged; and (3) strike through each characteristic or behavior that you think should be discouraged.

1. Adventurous, testing limits
2. Affectionate, loving
3. Altruistic, working for good of others
4. Asking questions about puzzling things
5. Attempting difficult tasks
6. Becoming preoccupied with tasks
7. Competitive, trying to win
8. Conforming
9. Considerate of others
10. Courageous in convictions
11. Courteous, polite
12. Critical of others
13. Curious, searching
14. Desirous of excelling
15. Determined, unflinching
16. Disturbing procedures and organization of the group
17. Doing work on time
18. Domineering, controlling
19. Emotionally sensitive
20. Energetic, vigorous
21. Fault-finding, objecting
22. Fearful, apprehensive
23. Feeling emotions strongly
24. Guessing, hypothesizing
25. Haughty and self-satisfied
26. Healthy
27. Independent in judgment
28. Independent in thinking
29. Industrious, busy
30. Intuitive
31. Liking to work alone
32. Neat and orderly
33. Negativistic, resistant
34. Never bored, always interested
35. Obedient, submissive to authority
36. Persistent, persevering
37. Physically strong
38. Popular, well-liked
39. Preferring complex tasks
40. Quiet, not talkative
41. Receptive to ideas of others
42. Refined, free of coarseness
43. Regressing occasionally, may be playful, childlike, etc.
44. Remembering well
45. Reserved
46. Self-assertive
47. Self-confident
48. Self-starting, initiating
49. Self-sufficient
50. Sense of beauty
51. Sense of humor
52. Sincere, earnest
53. Socially well-adjusted
54. Spirited in disagreement
55. Striving for distant goals
56. Stubborn, obstinate
57. Talkative
58. Thorough
59. Timid, shy, bashful
60. Truthful, even when it hurts
61. Unsophisticated, artless
62. Unwilling to accept things on mere say-so
63. Versatile, well-rounded
64. Visionary, idealistic
65. Willing to accept judgments of authorities
66. Willing to take risks

DEVELOPED BY E. PAUL TORRANCE

GEORGIA STUDIES OF CREATIVE BEHAVIOR, COLLEGE OF EDUCATION
THE UNIVERSITY OF GEORGIA
AUGUST 1967

Appendix B

What Happens when Teachers are Respectful of Unusual Questions and Ideas

The following are selected descriptions of actual experiences reported by teachers as to what happened when they attempted to reward the creative thinking of children.

Principle 1: Be Respectful of Unusual Questions

Incident 1: Would you turn Communist? (Grade 6)

Occasion: During social studies period, while discussing living conditions of the Russian people, one boy asked "Mr. _____,would you turn Communist if the Russians captured America?"

Immediate Teacher Reaction: Does he feel we eventually will be attacked by the Russians? Why?

Immediate Reaction of Class: General reaction—What would happen if America were attacked and captured?

Way Respect Shown for Question: The children really, seriously considered or thought about the question.

Effects: Your prediction?

Incident 2: Why do you need two rabbits to have little rabbits? (Grade 4)

Occasion: We had a rabbit in our classroom and the discussion was centered in it. The class was very much interested in the discussion. A boy asked, "Why do you need two rabbits to have little rabbits?" Everyone joined in and wanted to know.

Immediate Teacher Reaction: My immediate thought was, "I can't teach sex in school." My action was to laugh and casually change the subject.

Immediate Class Reaction: There was a keen interest in the question. I observed that a couple drew a little color.

Way Respect Shown for Question: I told the class that there are many questions asked that are good but hard to answer without going into research.

Effects: Your prediction?

Principle 2: Be Respectful of Imaginative Ideas

Incident 1:   *More mature behavior by "pretending?"* (Grade 1)

Occasion: As we were discussing rules and manners for first graders, one six-year-old boy said, "I am going to act like a doctor going to school all day."

Immediate Teacher Reaction: If you act like a doctor today, we'll have a perfect classroom.

Immediate Class Reaction: Others suggested that they all pretend to be a grown-up person.

Way Respect Shown: There was no ridicule, and all the children were encouraged to pretend to be someone special.

Effects: Your prediction?

Incident 2:   *The "Twilight Zone"* (Grade 1)

Occasion: I was introducing a poem, "February Twilight," and asked the class what "twilight" meant. One boy said that it meant "Twilight Zone." When asked what that meant, he said that it had something to do with the brain.

Immediate Teacher Reaction: I asked him how "Twilight Zone" made him feel, and he answered, "Kinda funny—like it's different," and then he seemed confused as to how to express himself. I then said that I liked his idea and that maybe we could think better if we knew what twilight was. When everyone seemed puzzled, I suggested it was a time of day. Several then immediately suggested "not really light," "almost night," "when the sun goes down," and so on.

Immediate Class Reaction: The class was very much interested and wanted to contribute *their* ideas to the vague idea that was given.

Way Respect Shown: I was very much interested in his ideas and encouraged others to contribute.

Effects: Your predictions?

Incident 3: Playing cowboy with a rope (Grade 3)

Occasion: We usually plan games before we go out for recess. Jerry suggested that we play cowboys with a rope that is usually used for jumping.

Immediate Teacher Reaction: Too much TV cowboy pictures. It was a dangerous thought.

Immediate Class Reaction: They went along with it.

Way Respect Shown: We discussed rope experts' ability to catch villains in movies and TV, or animals in rodeos.

Effects: Your prediction?

Incident 4:   Do male moths lay eggs? (Grades 4 and 5)

Occasion: A boy brought a cocoon to school. After two weeks, the moth hatched. We put the moth into a large glass container. The children read about moths in books. Through their reading, they learned that it was a male cecropia moth. Every morning, they would observe the moth carefully. Through their reading, they had learned that moths lay eggs. But morning after morning, no eggs. They couldn't understand why this moth didn't lay eggs. I passed no comment. I listened. Finally a boy said, "I know; it's a male, and males don't lay eggs." Another boy said, "Males do lay eggs."

Class Reaction: Some silly giggling among the fifth grade boys (above average ability group), as much as to say, "Don't you know?"

Teacher Reaction: Then I said, "I think I know what you mean. I think you mean that a female can't lay an egg alone." "That's right," said a boy, and there was some more silly laughter and uncomfortable behavior. I said, "I haven't heard it said that a male lays an egg. I had always heard or read that a male passes a seed to a female and then, after some time, the female produces its own kind."

Way Respect Shown: We talked about some of the animals that lay eggs and about the hatching of them.

Effects: Your predictions?

Selected References

ANDERSON, J. E. "The Nature of Abilities." *Talent and Education,* edited by E. Paul Torrance, pp. 9-31. Minneapolis: University of Minnesota Press, 1960.

ANDERSON, M. *Children of the South.* New York: Farrar, Straus & Giroux, 1966.

ANGLUND, J. W. *What Color Is Love?* New York: Harcourt, Brace & World, 1966.

APPLEGATE, M. *Helping Children Write.* Scranton, Pa.: International Textbook Company, 1949.

BARNARD, H., ed. *Papers on Froebel's Kindergarten, with Suggestions on Principles and Methods of Child Culture.* Syracuse, N. Y.: C. W. Bardeen, 1879.

BARTLETT, F. M. *Thinking.* New York: Basic Books, 1958.

BEREITER, C., and ENGLEMANN, S. *Teaching Disadvantaged Children in the Preschool.* Englewood Cliffs, N. J.: Prentice-Hall, 1966.

BERENSTAIN, J., and BERENSTAIN, S. *Inside, Outside, Upside Down.* New York: Random House, 1968.

BINET, A. *Les Idées Modernes sur les Enfants.* Paris: E. Flamarion, 1909.

BORAAS, J. *Teaching to Think.* New York: Macmillan Co., 1922.

BOWEN, H. C. *Froebel and Education through Self-Activity.* New York: Charles Scribner's Sons, 1906.

BRAITHWAITE, E. R. *To Sir, with Love.* Englewood Cliffs, N. J.: Prentice-Hall, 1959.

BROUDY, H. S. "Historic Exemplars of Teaching Method." *Handbook of Research on Teaching,* edited by N. L. Gage, pp. 1-43. Chicago: Rand McNally & Co., 1963.

BROWN, M. W. *The Color Kittens.* New York: Golden Press, 1958.

BRUCH, C. B. "A Proposed Rationale for the Identification and Development of the Gifted Disadvantaged." Athens, Ga.: Department of Educational Psychology, University of Georgia, 1969.

CATTELL, R. B. *The Culture-Free Intelligence Test.* Champaign, Ill.: Institute for Personality Assessment and Testing, 1949.

CIARDI, J. *I Met a Man.* (Record album) Cambridge, Mass.: Pathways of Sound, 1962.

CLYMER, T. *A Duck Is a Duck.* Boston: Ginn & Co., 1960. (a)

CLYMER, T. *Helicopters and Gingerbread*. Boston: Ginn & Co., 1969. (b)
CLYMER, T., and GATES, D. *May I Come In?* Boston: Ginn & Co., 1969.
CLYMER, T., and JONES, V. W. *Seven Is Magic*. Boston: Ginn & Co., 1969.
CLYMER, T., and NEFF, P. H. *How It Is Nowadays*. Boston: Ginn & Co., 1969.
COLES, R. *Dead End School*. Boston: Atlantic-Little, Brown & Co., 1968.
CREMIN, L. A. *The Transformation of the School*. New York: Vintage Books, Random House, 1961.
CUNNINGTON, B. F., and TORRANCE, E. P. *Imagi/Craft*. (Set of 10 albums and teacher guides) Boston: Ginn & Co., 1965.
DAVIS, A. *Social Class Influences on Learning*. Cambridge, Mass.: Harvard University Press, 1948.
DAVIS, A., and EELLS, K. *Davis-Eells Games*. New York: Harcourt, Brace & World, 1953.
DEUTSCH, M. *The Disadvantaged Child: Studies of the Social Environment and the Learning Process*. New York: Basic Books, 1967.
DREWS, E. M. "Beyond Curriculum." *Journal of Humanistic Psychology*, 1968; 8, pp. 97-112. (a)
DREWS, E. M. "Fernwood: A Free School." *Journal of Humanistic Psychology*, 1968, 8, pp. 113-122. (b)
DURRELL, D., and CHAMBERS, J. R. "Research in Thinking Abilities." *Reading Teacher*, 1958, 12, pp. 89-91.
EDDY, E. M. *Walk the White Line*. Garden City, N. Y.: Doubleday & Co., 1967.
EMBERLEY, E. *The Wing on a Flea*. Boston: Little, Brown & Co., 1961.
EMBERLEY, E. *Cock a Doodle Doo: A Book of Sounds*. Boston: Little, Brown & Co., 1964.
FISHER, A. *Listen, Rabbit*. New York: Thomas Y. Crowell Co., 1964.
FROEBEL, F. *Mother's Songs, Games, and Stories*. Translated by Frances and Emily Lord. London: William Rice; Chicago: Alice B. Stockham & Co., 1891.
———. *Pedagogics of the Kindergarten*. Translated by Josephine Jarvis. New York: Appleton-Century-Crofts, 1904.
FROST, J. L., and HAWKES, G. R., eds. *The Disadvantaged Child: Issues and Innovations*. Boston: Houghton Mifflin Co., 1966.
GLASSER, W. *Schools without Failure*. New York: Harper & Row, 1969.
GOLDMAN, R. J. *Breakthrough*. London: Routledge & Kegan Paul, Ltd., 1968.
GOTKIN, L. G., and MASSA, N. "Programmed Instruction and the Academically Gifted: The Effects of Creativity and Teacher Behavior on Programmed Instruction with Young Learners." New York: Center for Programmed Instruction, 1963. (Mimeographed)
GREEN, M. M. *Is It Hard? Is It Easy?* New York: William R. Scott, 1960.
GUILFORD, J. P. "Intelligence: 1965 Model." *American Psychologist*, 1966, 21, pp. 20-26.
———. *The Nature of Human Intelligence*. New York: McGraw-Hill Book Co., 1967.
———. *Intelligence, Creativity, and Their Educational Implications*. San Diego: Robert R. Knapp, 1968.
HART, L. *The Classroom Disaster*. New York: Teachers College Press, Teachers College, Columbia University, 1969.

HERNDON, J. *The Way It Spozed to Be.* New York: Simon & Schuster, 1965.
HOWE, F. "Untaught Teachers and Improbable Poets." *Saturday Review,* March 15, 1969, 52(11), pp. 60-62, 79.
HUNT, J. McV. *Intelligence and Experience.* New York: Ronald Press Co., 1961.
———. "Environment, Development, and Scholastic Achievement." *Social Class, Race, and Psychological Development,* edited by M. Deutsch, I. Katz, and A. R. Jensen, pp. 115-174. New York: Holt, Rinehart & Winston, 1968.
HUTCHINSON, W. L. "Creative and Productive Thinking in the Classroom." Doctoral dissertation, University of Utah, Salt Lake City, 1963.
KAUFMAN, B. *Up the Down Staircase.* Englewood Cliffs, N. J.: Prentice-Hall, 1964.
KENDALL, R. *White Teacher in a Black School.* Chicago: Henry Regnery Co., 1964.
KOHL, H. *36 Children.* New York: New American Library, 1967.
KOZOL, J. *Death at an Early Age.* Boston: Houghton Mifflin Co., 1967.
LAMORISSE, A. *The Red Balloon.* Garden City, N.Y.: Doubleday & Co., 1956.
LEIGH, M., and DORION, J. *Man of La Mancha.* (Record album) New York: Kapp Records, 1966.
MacDONALD, J. B., and RATHS, J. D. "Should We Group by Creative Abilities?" *Elementary School Journal,* 1964, 65, pp. 137-142.
MASLOW, A. H. "Goals of Humanistic Education." (Tape recording) Esalen Institute, Big Sur, Calif., 1968.
McCONNELL, T. R. "Discovery vs. Authoritative Identification in the Learning of Children." *University of Iowa Studies in Education,* 1934, 9(5), pp. 13-62.
MEEKER, M. N. *The Structure of Intellect: Its Interpretation and Uses.* Columbus, Ohio: Charles E. Merrill Publishing Co., 1969.
MONTESSORI, M. *Spontaneous Activity in Education.* (Reprinted from 1917 edition) Cambridge, Mass.: Robert Bentley, 1964.
MORENO, J. L. *Psychodrama: First Volume.* New York: Beacon House, 1946.
MOUSTAKAS, C. E. *Psychotherapy with Children.* New York: Harper & Row, 1959.
MUNARI, B. *The Elephant's Wish.* Cleveland: World Publishing Co., 1959.
MURPHY, G. *Human Potentialities.* New York: Basic Books, 1958.
MYERS, R. E., and TORRANCE, E. P. *Invitations to Thinking and Doing.* Boston: Ginn & Co., 1964.
———. *Can You Imagine?* Boston: Ginn & Co., 1965. (a)
———. *Invitations to Speaking and Writing Creatively.* Boston: Ginn & Co., 1965. (b)
———. *For Those Who Wonder.* Boston: Ginn & Co., 1966. (a)
———. *Plots, Puzzles, and Ploys.* Boston: Ginn & Co., 1966 (b)
NEWELL, A.; SHAW, J. C.; and SIMON, H. A. "The Processes of Creative Thinking." *Contemporary Approaches to Creative Thinking,* edited by H. E. Gruber, G. Terrell, ana M. Wertheimer, pp. 65-66. New York: Atherton Press, 1962.
O'NEILL, M. *Hailstones and Halibut Bones.* Garden City, N.Y.: Doubleday & Co., 1961.

OSBORN, A. F. *Applied Imagination*. 3d ed. New York: Charles Scribner's Sons, 1963.

PARNES, S. J. *Creative Behavior Guidebook*. New York: Charles Scribner's Sons, 1967.

PARNES, S. J., and MEADOW, A. "Effects of 'Brainstorming' Instructions on Creative Problem Solving by Trained and Untrained Subjects." *Journal of Educational Psychology*, 1959, 50, pp. 171-176.

———. "Evaluation of Persistence of Effects Produced by Trained and Untrained Subjects." *Psychological Reports*, 1960, 7, pp. 357-361.

PESTALOZZI, J. H. *How Gertrude Teaches Her Children*. Translated by L. E. Holland and F. C. Turner. Syracuse, N.Y.: Bardeen, 1894.

RIESSMAN, F. *The Culturally Deprived Child*. New York: Harper & Row, 1962.

ROGERS, V. R. "History for the Elementary School Child." *Phi Delta Kappan*, 1962, 44, pp. 132-135.

ROSENTHAL, R., and JACOBSON, L. *Pygmalion in the Classroom*. New York: Holt, Rinehart & Winston, 1968.

SALISBURY, K. *Tell a Tall Tale*. New York: Western Publishing Co., 1966.

SAMSON, R. W. *The Mind Builder: A Self-Teaching Guide to Creative Thinking and Analysis*. New York: E. P. Dutton & Co., 1965.

SELYE, H. "The Gift of Basic Research." *The Yearbook of Education*, edited by G. Z. Bereday and J. A. Lauwerys, pp. 399-408. New York: Harcourt, Brace & World, 1962.

SHAHN, B. "On Painting." *The Creative Mind and Method*. Cambridge, Mass.: WGBH-FM, 1959, pp. 20-21.

SHIRREFF, E. "Educational Principles of the Kindergarten." *Education*, 1881, 1, pp. 425-432.

SINGER, J. L. "Exploring Man's Imaginative World." *Teachers College Record*, 1964, 66, pp. 165-179.

SMITH, R. M. "The Relationship of Creativity to Social Class." (Final Report CRP 2250) Washington, D. C.: Bureau of Research, United States Office of Education, 1965.

STOLUROW, L. M. "Social Impact of Programmed Instruction: Aptitudes and Abilities Revisted." *Educational Technology*, edited by J. P. De Cecco, pp. 348-355. New York: Holt, Rinehart & Winston, 1964.

TABA, H., and ELKINS, D. *Teaching Strategies for the Culturally Disadvantaged*. Chicago: Rand McNally & Co., 1966.

TAYLOR, C. W. "Cultivating New Talents: A Way to Reach the Educationally Deprived." *Journal of Creative Behavior*, 1968, 2, pp. 83-90.

TERMAN, L. M. *Mental and Physical Traits of a Thousand Gifted Children*. Stanford, Calif.: Stanford University Press, 1925.

———. "The Discovery and Encouragement of Exceptional Talent." *American Psychologist*, 1954, 9, pp. 221-230.

TORRANCE, E. P. *Guiding Creative Talent*. Englewood Cliffs, N. J.: Prentice-Hall, 1962.

———. *Education and the Creative Potential*. Minneapolis: University of Minnesota Press, 1963.

———. *Rewarding Creative Behavior*. Englewood Cliffs, N. J.: Prentice-Hall, 1965. (a)

———. "Different Ways of Learning for Different Kinds of Children." *Mental Health and Achievement*, edited by E. P. Torrance and R. D. Strom, pp. 253-262. New York: John Wiley & Sons, 1965. (b)

———. "Motivating Children with School Problems." *Mental Health and Achievement*, edited by E. P. Torrance and R. D. Strom, pp. 338-353. New York: John Wiley & Sons, 1965. (c)

———. *The Torrance Tests of Creative Thinking: Norms-Technical Manual (Research Edition)*. Princeton, N. J.: Personnel Press, 1966.

———. *Understanding the Fourth Grade Slump in Creative Thinking*. Washington, D. C.: Bureau of Research, United States Office of Education, 1967. (Final Report on CRP 994) (a)

———. "Nurture of Creative Talents." *Theory into Practice*, 1967, 5, pp. 168-174. (b)

———. "Independent Study as an Instructional Tool." *Theory into Practice*, 1967, 5, pp. 217-224. (c)

———. "Comparative Studies of Stress-Seeking in the Imaginative Stories of Preadolescents in Twelve Different Subcultures." *Why Man Takes Chances*, edited by S. Z. Klausner, pp. 195-233. Garden City, N.Y.: Doubleday & Co., 1968. (a)

———. "Must Pre-Primary Educational Stimulation Be Incompatible with Creative Development?" *Creativity at Home and in School*, edited by F. E. Williams, pp. 54-73. St. Paul: Macalester Creativity Project, Macalester College, 1968. (b)

———. *Dimensions of Early Learning: Creativity*. San Rafael, Calif.: Dimensions Publishing Co., 1969.

TORRANCE, E. P., and FORTSON, L. R. "Creativity among Young Children and the Creative-Aesthetic Approach." *Education*, 1968, 89, pp. 27-30.

TORRANCE, E. P.; FORTSON, L. R.; and DIENER, C. "Creative-Aesthetic Ways of Developing Intellectual Skills among Five-Year-Olds." *Journal of Research and Development in Education*, 1968, 1(3), pp. 58-69.

TORRANCE, E. P., and GUPTA, R. *Development and Evaluation of Recorded Programmed Experiences in Creative Thinking in Fourth Grade*. Minneapolis: Bureau of Educational Research, University of Minnesota, 1964.

TORRANCE, E. P., and HARMON, J. A. "Effects of Memory, Evaluative, and Creative Reading Sets on Test Performance." *Journal of Educational Psychology*, 1961, 52, pp. 207-214.

TORRANCE, E. P., and TORRANCE, P. "Softest, Shortest, Slowest, Smallest . . ." *Music for Primaries*, 1969, 3(2), pp. 22-24.

TOYNBEE, A. "Our Neglected Creative Minority." *Old Oregon*, September-October, 1965, 45(2), pp. 30-32.

UNGERER, T. *Snail, Where Are You?* New York: Harper & Row, 1962.

WITT, G. *The Life Enrichment Activity Program: A Brief History*. New Haven, Conn.: LEAP, Inc., 363 Dixwell Ave., 1968. (Mimeographed.)

WITTE, P., and WITTE, E. *The Touch Me Book*. New York: Western Publishing Co., 1961.

WOLFF, J. *Let's Imagine Being Places*. New York: E. P. Dutton & Co., 1961. (a)

———. *Let's Imagine Thinking Up Things*. New York: E. P. Dutton & Co., 1961. (b)

———. *Let's Imagine Sounds*. New York: E. P. Dutton & Co., 1962.

Author Index

Subject Index

Absorption, 19-20, 33
Acceptance of limitations, 8
Achievement orientation, 112
Activities, abstract-concrete, 37; after reading, 63; before reading, 63; during reading, 63; easy-difficult, 36; sequences of, 36; suggested, 81
Addiction to reading, 110
Adults as sources of help, 76
Alternate consequences, 46-49
Alternate outcomes of stories, 50
Alternate uses, 46
Alternative solutions, 48
Ambiguities, 7-8, 51, 67, 83
Analogies, 7, 14, 47, 53, 87
Analysis, training in, 43
Answer, correct or best, 86
Anticipation, 7-8, 60, 62, 65, 68
Art, 6, 42, 80, 86, 109
Assessment instruments, 91
Attempting difficult and dangerous tasks, 17-18
Attention span, 97-98
Attitude toward what is read, 58
Auditory imagery, 58
Authority, learning by, 1, 2, 13, 15, 36
Auxiliary ego, 65-66
Availability of knowledge, 61
Awareness, by recording, predicting, and checking predictions, 29; of complex sounds, 46; of gaps in information, 68, 83-84; of a person's individuality, 26; of a problem, 68, 75, 83; of pupils' potential, 84; through heightened consciousness, 30; through interpersonal reaction, 29

Beauty, deprivation of, 112
Behavior, alternative causes of, 48
Brainstorming, 51-52, 69, 76, 84, 97, 101-102
B-values, 112
Byrd, R., 18

Cats and learning, 14
Causal thinking, 50, 58, 100
Challenge, responding to, 18; of task, 31
Cinquains, 52, 97
Classroom meetings, 107
Co-action, 65
Color, manipulation of, 41
Columbus, C., 57
Combinations, new, 42, 45; of people and animals, 42
Communication of discovery, 2
Competence, 100
Complex tasks, preference for, 18
Component skills, 52-53
Concern about a problem, 69, 84
Conclusions, differentiated from hypotheses, 52
Concrete objects, 104
Conformity to norms, 21
Connectedness, 33, 37
Consequences, 50, 58
Construction of objects, 43, 80
Constructive response, 84